# L'Art de la Table

ISBN 978-94-026-0059-9

© 2015  Text and design: Gintare Marcel
© 2015  Photography: Gintare Marcel
© 2015  First published in hardback by Aerial Media Company, Tiel, The Netherlands

Editor: Danny Guinan, Wordforword
Pre-Production Producer: Teo van Gerwen

www.aerialmediacom.nl
www.facebook.com/Aerialmediacompany

The moral rights of Gintare Marcel to be identified as the author and photographer of this work has been asserted in accordance with the Copyright, Designs and Patents Act of 1988.

Aerial Media Company bv.
Postbus 6088
4000 HB Tiel, The Netherlands

# L'ART DE LA TABLE

*taste of the Mediterranean*

GINTARE MARCEL

AERIAL MEDIA COMPANY

To my dearest ones, and all
seeking to live delicious lives.

# Contents

# Before you begin cooking

*"One cannot think well, love well, sleep well, if one has not dined well."*
*Virginia Woolf*

Buried in the depths of the Castilian language lies a word of special sense and meaning: Duende. It refers to the mysterious power of art to move one deeply, to shake the soul to its core, bring a tear to the eye, and bring forth inspiration long since forgotten.

Wise men have long argued that music dance and poetry are the grandest cradles of duende. But for me, each table, each plate, where spoonfuls of taste and texture await and where stories and scents mingle and fuse in the air waiting to tell a tale or two of their own, is duende - a muse like no other.

I have had a lifelong love affair with food, with its ability to awaken the senses, carry you across the earth with a single bite and bring people together. A love affair that began with indulging and savoring every plate in sight and that in time grew into a quest for the perfect fusion of flavors, textures, swooning scents and secrets.

I was born and raised in the beautiful country of Lithuania, a land where the ingredients of our meals grew only a stone's throw away in the garden, where each repast was freshly prepared and wholesome seasonal ingredients were valued above all others. Summers were for preserving fruits and berries, and when snow blankets covered the fields, pickles and homemade jams were a frequent presence on the table. Gatherings of friends and family were common and loud, and food always seemed to bring everyone together.

This slightly old-fashioned way of life and cooking is at the heart of what I do, along with the frequently forgotten principles of moderation.

Through my many journeys I fell in love with the diversity of the Mediterranean. I became enchanted with the ritual of slowing down, sipping apéro whilst watching the world rush by, and allowing all daily worries to subside, not forgetting, of course, the whole new world of flavors that opened up before me. Although eating has always been and still is my greatest talent, my trips to my husband's home in Provence soon ignited a passion to create food for and inspire others.

L'art de la Table is written in the spirit of gathering, the art of slow living and engaging with food, and its flavors guide one to the shores of Mediterranean. In our ever-busy world, there are lessons to be learned from those who consider the dinner table a kind of altar and are always able to find the time to sit down to a delicious meal.

# ❧ What lies within ❧

When I think of the Mediterranean I think of merging cultures, crumbling buildings, overgrown ports and abandoned tonnaras. I think of hollow streets and pavements where the stones have been etched deep into the earth and have more than a story or two to tell of their own.

I think of endless shorelines bursting with spectacular flavors, from the verveine-scented Provence to the rose-imbued Eastern coast. Where the purity and simplicity of Italian cuisine in Sicily blends with exotic Moorish flavors and the intricacy of French cuisine flourishes in Occitania, the ancient province in France whose history extends across the Spanish and Italian borders. Where the sea still hides the culinary gems of thousands of islands.

Such a melting pot of cultures holds far more than any single book can hope to embody. This book is inspired by my own journeys, age-old traditions and the merging of ancient cultures. But most of all it recounts my passion for the food that I love to eat and share with others.

# Kitchen secrets

I have always seen cooking as an art of sorts, where a fine line exists between the good and the great. Perhaps, like a map steering a way through city streets, a recipe can only guide you to your destination and always leaves you space to wander and take a few steps of your own choosing. So, apart from the recipes themselves, there are a couple of other things that are worth keeping in mind.

Tasting is of the utmost importance; in fact it is the essence of cooking. We use it not only to discover whether something decent will await us at the end of the process, but also tells us that a zucchini tastes different in Italy than it does in the Netherlands or France. The same can be said for almost every other ingredient you will ever lay your hands on, and these differences, however small they might be, will call for adjustments, even if only as miniscule as adding an extra pinch of thyme or sugar. So, any time you find yourself in the kitchen, the trick is to taste and taste, and taste again ad infinitum. Nothing bad has ever come out of it, unless of course you're not the cook and only trying to steal a morsel or two before dinner - always a potentially dangerous affair.

It should also go without saying that reading a recipe through (twice) before even thinking of starting is imperative and can literally make or break a meal.

Apart from the ingredients, it is also worthwhile saying something about kitchen equipment. I am not a fan of fancy kitchen gadgets and believe that a few good knives and pans can go a long way. But if I were to recommend a few utensils that are worth investing in, then the first would be a food processor (preferably with blender). It can do everything from making dough to blending sauces and mixing mash. I would not survive in the kitchen without mine.

I use immense amounts of zests in my dishes, so in addition to stocking up on lemons and oranges it's worthwhile getting a **microplane**, which is not only very efficient, it will also save time on cleaning. You will find that it quickly becomes an indispensable weapon.

A **hand-held** or **standing mixer** also comes in handy, even if you are not an avid baker, as does a **griddle (grill) pan**. These things I consider to be absolutely essential.

For the rest, it all comes down to getting your hands on fresh seasonal and whole ingredients (especially when it comes to dairy) and perhaps making a little space on the windowsill to grow some fresh herbs. They truly make all the difference between the good and the great and require far less effort than you might think.

# Morning hour

I always remember mornings in Sicily with great fondness, and not only because sitting at the table with the sea on one side and orange and lemon groves on the other is my idea of sheer bliss, with the heat slowly reaching into your bones even at the earliest hour. In Sicily, morning hour is a special one; with a steaming cappuccino there will always be a freshly baked brioscia siciliana (not to be confused with the French brioche) and, if you're lucky, a wonderful almond or lemon granita. The contrast of fresh ice with rich brioche is as unlikely as it is marvelous. For a sweet lover like me, there is not much left to yearn for when I can start my day with a generous scoop of ice cream. When not in Sicily, I usually supplement my morning cappuccino with crispy granola or a so-called breakfast cake, or perhaps a bowl of steaming oats. A hearty breakfast, in my mind, is a must at the start of the day and I'd like to invite you to try out some of my favorite treats, all of which have a dessert-like quality in addition to a healthy touch.

# Hazelnuts and breakfast - the Sicilian way

Almond granita is one of the most popular treats for breakfast in Sicily, but I find the subtle taste of almonds becomes barely negligible when it has been made into milk. And even though almond granita is incredibly delicious, it comes nowhere close to one made out of hazelnuts. Hazelnuts, in my humble opinion, are a much underused and wonderful treat, undeservedly trailing far behind almonds in the popularity stakes. They have such a profound taste and hold their flavor so firmly that once they have been turned into a thick creamy milk the result is more like a dessert than a casual nut milk. Anything made using it tastes like pure heaven. When autumn comes and the nostalgia for sunny days sets in, I usually find myself making hazelnut milk from fresh hazelnuts and enjoying granita with Sicilian brioche the next day for breakfast. This 'brioscia siciliana' is rich and fairly dense, and has a healthy dose of Marsala wine running through its veins. I make mine the Catania way, with a pinch of saffron for a serious treat, but you can also use vanilla or a drop of orange blossom water instead if you prefer.

...

## Hazelnut milk

Time | 15 mins / freeze for 3-4 hours    Servings | 2

130 g/5 oz hazelnuts, soaked overnight

5 dates, pitted and soaked in hot water for 5 minutes

⅓ vanilla pod

500-750 ml/2-3 cups water

In a blender, whizz the hazelnut, dates and vanilla together with the water (start with 2 cups and add more depending on taste).

Let it stand for 10-15 minutes to infuse, then strain through a double cheesecloth.

It will keep in the fridge for about 3 days.

Note: to make chocolate hazelnut milk, add 2 tablespoons of cacao nibs when blending.

Pour the hazelnut milk into a shallow dish and transfer to the freezer for at least 3-4 hours or overnight. Remove from the freezer and to make the granita use a fork to gradually scratch out the frozen hazelnut milk.

# Sicilian brioche

Time | 35 mins    Servings | 4

60 ml/¼ cup milk, warm
pinch of saffron
1 tbsp honey
1 tbsp Marsala wine
300 g/10½ oz/2 cups finely ground
   durum wheat flour
7 g instant yeast
50 g/¼ cup sugar
pinch of salt
2 eggs, beaten
120 g/8 tbsp butter, cubed

**Egg wash**
1 egg
1 tbsp water

Mix the milk and saffron and set aside to soak for 10 minutes.

Mix the honey with the Marsala wine and set aside.

In a bowl, whisk the flour, yeast, sugar and salt together and stir in the warm milk, followed by the eggs. You can do this by hand or with a mixer (dough hook attached).

Stir in the butter, little by little, and once all the butter is incorporated, slowly stir in the Marsala and honey. Knead the dough until it no longer sticks to the sides of the bowl (about 3-5 minutes). Cover the dough with a tea towel and leave to rise in a warm spot for about an hour until it has doubled in size.

Give it another quick knead, cover with plastic wrap, and leave in the fridge overnight.

Preheat the oven to 200°C/400°F. and line a tray with baking paper.

Divide the dough into 12-14 equal parts (reserving two parts for the topping) and shape them into balls. Place them on the tray, leaving enough space to rise. Out of the reserved dough, shape a few smaller balls and press them on top of the others. Cover and leave to rise for about 1½ hours.

To make the egg wash, beat the egg with the water and gently brush onto each brioche. Bake the brioche for about 15 minutes, depending on the oven. Serve warm with granita.


# Hazelnut smoothie

Time | 5 mins    Servings | 2

250 ml/1 cup hazelnut milk
1 frozen banana (2 hours in the
   freezer is enough)
1 orange, juice only
1 tbsp chia seeds (optional)
1 tsp raw cacao powder or 1 tbsp
   cacao nibs

It would certainly be a crime of some sort not to try making this smoothie at least once in your life, not only because it is one of my favorite morning and afternoon treats but also because it is certain to steal your heart with its soothing hazelnut, chocolate and banana notes.

For two small portions or one greedy helping you will need to blend together 250 ml/1 cup hazelnut milk, 1 frozen banana (must be frozen), the juice of 1 orange, 1tbsp chia seeds and 1 tsp raw cacao powder or 1 tbsp cacao nibs. Serve immediately.

# Chocolate hazelnut granola

A jar of homemade granola occupies pride of place on my shelves. For a chocolate lover like me there is no greater pleasure than starting the day with a bowl full of chocolate, preferably a healthy one. Sweetened only with honey and with a touch of milk or yogurt, this granola tastes like crunchy Nutella and will keep you full until lunchtime comes. Granola itself will keep for at least a week in an airtight container - if you can resist the temptation to nibble at it in the meantime...

Time | 30 mins    Servings | 6-8

2 tbsp coconut oil
450 g/½ lb oats
250 g/9 oz hazelnuts, chopped
150 g/5 oz almonds, chopped
3 tbsp cacao powder
60 ml/¼ cup coffee or water
4-6 tbsp honey

Preheat the oven to 160°C/320°F and line a tray with baking paper.

In a large non-stick pan, heat the coconut oil and fry the oats for 2-3 minutes, stirring all the time.

Tip in the nuts, stir in the cacao powder, thoroughly coating everything, and pour over the coffee or water. Adding liquid helps the oats to absorb the cacao powder better.

Finally, coat the granola with honey, spread it evenly onto the baking paper and bake for 15-20 minutes.

If, after baking, the granola is still too moist, reduce the heat to 75°C/165°F and leave until it's dry and crunchy.

Serve with milk or yogurt.

◄▲►

Variation | When fall comes knocking at the door I can never resist adding the flavors of autumn and apple pie to my morning granola. Roasted apple adds a wonderful touch, but if you are short on time fresh ones will work great too. To make an autumn 'apple pie-like' granola, substitute the cacao for 1 tbsp of cinnamon and the coffee for the juice and zest of 1 orange. To top off this granola, add 2 apples - peeled, cored and sliced - to a shallow dish, pour over the juice of another orange, place a cinnamon stick in the center and sprinkle with 1 tsp brown sugar. Bake for 15 minutes. Serve with crunchy granola and plenty of natural yogurt.

# Breakfast almond cheesecake

*The origins of this particular cheesecake are far removed from the Mediterranean coast. In fact, it was one of the staples in my household when I was growing up and it was frequently served for breakfast, lunch and even dinner; a multipurpose sort of treat with very modest sugar quantities and lots of extra possibilities. These days I prefer it for breakfast above all else, and with a touch of orange blossom water, orange zest and fennel seeds it is simply irresistible, though it does call for something fresh on the side. Just about any fruit sauce works well here, but orange blossom water and strawberries are a match made in heaven..*

Time | 50 mins    Servings | 4

500 g/18 oz ricotta or fine cottage
 cheese
4 eggs, separated
2 tbsp sugar
30 g/2 tbsp butter (room
 temperature, diced) plus extra for
 greasing the baking tin
1 tsp fennel seeds, toasted and ground
1 orange zest
1 tbsp orange blossom water
6 tbsp almond flour
pinch of salt
almond flakes to finish (optional)

**Fresh strawberry sauce**
200 g/7 oz strawberries
1-2 tsp powder sugar
dash of lemon juice

Preheat the oven to 200°C/400°F.

Beat the egg yolks and sugar until pale, then beat in the butter and stir in the zest, fennel seeds, orange blossom water, ricotta and almond flour.

Beat the egg whites with a pinch of salt until stiff peaks begin to form and gently fold ⅓ of the egg whites into the cheese mixture, followed by the rest. Be careful not to stir too much.

Pour the batter into a greased tin (any baking tin will do) and bake for 25-30 minutes. To check if the cheesecake is ready, pierce it with a toothpick - it should come out clean.

To make the strawberry sauce, blend the strawberries with the sugar and lemon juice; check for taste.

Serve the cheesecake warm with fresh strawberry sauce.

# Berry and cacao nibs breakfast cake

*I do fancy the idea of having cake for breakfast immensely, and in the arena of healthy breakfast cakes this one has no equal. Here oats are baked with scrumptious amounts of berries and chocolate (if desired), transforming your humble baked oats into something more festive and weekend-like.*

Time | 40 mins    Servings | 2 - 4

3 eggs

250 ml/1 cup milk (dairy, nut or
   coconut)

3 tbsp honey

pinch of salt

2 tsp vanilla extract

120 g/4 oz oat flakes

70 g/2 ½ oz almond flour or regular
   flour

1 tsp baking powder

butter for greasing

250 g/9 oz mixed berries

2 tbsp cacao nibs or chocolate chips
   (optional)

2 tbsp almond flakes (optional)

yogurt, for serving

Pre heat the oven to 200°C/400°F.

Beat the eggs with the milk, honey, salt and vanilla extract. Stir in the oats, flour and baking powder. Set aside.

Grease a baking tin (any baking tin will do) and throw in the berries and cacao nibs (or chocolate chips). Pour over the batter evenly and top with almond flakes.

Bake for 25 minutes, depending on the oven; a toothpick inserted into the cake should come out clean when ready.

Serve the cake warm and with some yogurt on top if you like.

Variation | Make a healthy chocolate cake for breakfast by adding 2 tbsp of unsweetened cacao powder and replacing the berries and cacao nibs with 2 apples - peeled and sliced into wedges.

# Saffron oats with caramelized pear

It took me a lifetime to learn to love and appreciate porridge, although admittedly even today the name still does not sound overly appealing and doesn't do any justice to oats, which take on any flavor they encounter perfectly. Just a touch of cinnamon or vanilla will enhance any dish of this sort, but this particular one comes soaked in saffron, cardamom and cinnamon-spiced almond milk, and adorned with honey-grilled pears so you can start your day to the strains of a symphony of aromas and flavors. Saffron is a little pricey but worth indulging in when a healthy but festive breakfast is called for, and this one is most certainly the kind guilt-free treat that can convert any oat-hater into a swooning lover.

Time | 15 mins     Servings | 2

1 conference pear
1 tbsp honey and extra for drizzling
1 tsp lemon juice
140 g/ 5 oz regular oats
250 ml/ 1 cup almond milk or any
    other milk (dairy, coconut)
pinch of salt
pinch of saffron
pinch of cardamom
pinch of cinnamon
1/ 4 tsp vanilla extract

Turn the oven grill on.
Peel, halve and core the pear, and place on a tray lined with aluminum foil. Drizzle with a little honey and lemon juice and place under the grill for 10-15 minutes.
Bring the oats with the milk and spices to the boil and simmer for about 7-10 minutes. Once they are done, remove from the heat and stir in the honey.
Serve immediately with caramelized pears.

Variations | Porridge can also be made with just a cup of blueberries or caramelized bananas on top (halved bananas brushed with honey and sprinkled with cinnamon 5-10 minutes under a hot grill).

# Lavender and rosemary scones

*I have a weak spot for this British classic, especially when it takes so little time from whisking to table. All it requires is tossing all the ingredients together and a little love in the oven, and a flaky pastry for breakfast soon awaits you. Served with whipped cream and jam they are perfect for teatime, too, but nothing can beat the early morning scent of freshly baked pastry that lingers in the air, evoking memories of Provence. My favorite scones are spiked with lavender and rosemary, bringing together earthy and flowery notes in a little pastry that makes mornings just that little bit more special. But scones can also be baked plain, or with lemon, vanilla, orange or just about any other fruit or berry.*

Time | 35 mins    Servings | 4

250 g/9 oz/1⅔ cups flour
3 tbsp light brown sugar
pinch of salt
1 tsp baking powder
½ tsp baking soda
1 tbsp fresh chopped rosemary
1½ tsp ground lavender buds
60 g/4 tbsp chilled unsalted butter, cut into cubes
160 ml/⅔ cup buttermilk plus extra for brushing before baking
natural yogurt to serve

**Strawberry and Crème de Cassis jam**
150 g/5½ oz sliced strawberries
1 tbsp honey
2 tbsp Crème de Cassis

Preheat the oven to 200°C/400°F.

In a food processor or a bowl, mix together the flour, sugar, salt, baking powder, soda, rosemary and lavender. Add the butter and blend for a few seconds until it starts to resemble breadcrumbs (10 seconds in a food processor or by rubbing the ingredients together between your fingers for a few minutes).

Mixing at a low speed, stir in the buttermilk and continue to mix until the dough becomes sticky. It should be quite wet but still easy to handle. Place on a lightly floured surface, roll around in the flour just enough to coat it (makes it easier to handle) and pat into a disc about 15 cm/6 inches wide. Divide into 6-8 wedges or use a cutter to cut out circles.

Place the scones about 1-2 cm apart on a baking tray lined with baking paper and brush each one with the extra buttermilk. Bake for about 10-15 minutes until firm. Scones should be pale gold on top and darker on the bottom.

While the scones are baking, make the jam. In a small saucepan, combine the strawberries, honey and crème de cassis. Bring to the boil and continue to cook until reduced by ⅔ or half and has a jam-like consistency. Set aside.

Serve the scones hot with fresh jam and yogurt.

◂▴▸

*Tip* | *There's no need to buy a whole pack of buttermilk. Simply stir 1 tablespoon of fresh lemon juice or white wine vinegar into a cup/250ml of full-fat milk and allow for it to stand about 10 minutes. Voila, homemade buttermilk.*

# Apéro

There is a sacred practice in Provence and neighboring regions that the locals call "Apéro".
It is more a ritual than a practice and one for which people are never reluctant to make time. In rare cases it
can actually take up more time than the meal itself. Sometimes the ritual even begins in the hours following
breakfast in the form of a Mauresque, a popular cocktail in the south of France made out of orgeat syrup,
Pastis and water. As the day grows older, the orgeat syrup often vanishes mysteriously, leaving just Pastis
diluted with water - the most quintessential apéro in the south of France. Pastis is such a staple commodity in
these parts that one cannot but sense it lingering permanently in the air during endless summer celebrations.
This drink is the preferred choice of those who adore the flavor of anise, and if you do not, the locals will swear
that after drinking it for a while you will like it as much as they do. I have never reached this level of adoration
myself and my personal preference lies firmly with kir royal or muscat. However, I do appreciate the languid
way of life and the time that is set aside, almost religiously, for "Apéro", while simultaneously nibbling upon
the fabulous delicacies of the south.

# Kir royal

My favorite cocktail for kicking off an evening.

Time | 1 min    Servings | 1

1 part Crème De Cassis
4-5 parts Champagne or Prosecco

Pour the liquor into a tall glass or champagne flute and top up with chilled bubbly. Serve immediately.

# Grilled fig, goat's cheese and caramelized onion bruschetta

*Figs are wonderful additions to both sweet and savory dishes and often work superbly as a bridge between both. This bruschetta occupies the thin line between both of these worlds, with the sweetness of the figs and onions contrasting with the freshness of thyme and the creamy nature of goat's cheese. This is without doubt my favorite way of enjoying fresh figs and it is usually a big hit even with those who don't fancy them as much as I do. These lovely bruschettas can be prepared easily in advance, but it is those few minutes under the grill just before serving that make them extra special, when the figs become almost jam-like and blend with the melted goat's cheese.*

Time | 30 mins     Servings | 6

30 g/2 tbsp butter

8 large onions, halved and thinly sliced

a few sprigs of fresh thyme

2 garlic cloves, lightly crushed

1 tbsp brown sugar

salt and freshly ground pepper

1 ciabatta, sliced

200 g/7 oz fresh goat's cheese

10 very ripe figs, each cut into 4-8 wedges

Melt the butter in a saucepan and cook the onions with the thyme and garlic for 15-20 minutes on a very low heat. Stir in the sugar, season with salt and pepper, and continue to cook for another 5 minutes until the onions have fully caramelized. Remove the thyme and garlic.

Heat a griddle pan until smoking hot and quickly grill the ciabatta slices on both sides.

Turn the oven grill on.

Spread the caramelized onions on the ciabatta slices, crumble over the goat's cheese, add the fig wedges and sprinkle a little fresh thyme on top. Place the bruschetta under a hot grill for 2-3 minutes and serve immediately.

# Sicilian caponata

*Of all the wonderful things I have brought back from Sicily over the years, the caponata is surely in my top three, alongside my being proposed to and subsequently married on this gorgeous island. It is a quite deceptive dish. At first sight it looks rather mushy and unattractive, but there is nothing quite like the layers of flavor that lie in wait within. In Sicily, every town, village and even household has its own variation on the fabulous caponata and everyone will stubbornly insist that their way is the only way. The best caponatas, in my opinion, are those that really push the boundaries of sweet and sour, while the addition of nuts here gives both texture and a balanced flavor.*

*Time* | 45 mins     *Servings* | 4-6

2 large eggplants, diced
120 ml/½ cup sunflower oil
15g/½ oz almonds
15g/½ oz pistachios
15g/½ oz pine nuts
2 tbsp extra virgin olive oil
1 onion, chopped
700 g/2 cups tomato passata
1 tbsp unsalted capers, washed and
    patted dry
3 tsp sugar
salt and freshly ground pepper
2 tbsp red wine vinegar
a few handfuls of basil leaves,
    chopped
toasted bread to serve

Fry the eggplant in sunflower oil until golden brown, then place them on a paper towel to absorb any excess oil. You may need to do this in two batches.

Toast all of the nuts in a dry frying pan and crush them up.

Heat a little olive oil in a pan and fry the onion on a medium heat until soft. Stir in the tomato passata, nuts, capers and sugar. Season with salt and pepper and then add the fried eggplant. Stir well and leave to simmer for about 15 minutes. Turn the heat up, add the vinegar and cook for 3 more minutes. Taste and add more salt and pepper if needed. If it seems too sour, add a little more sugar.

Just before serving, stir in the fresh basil; serve the caponata with toasted bread and a dry white wine.

*Tip* | Caponata can even be made a day or two in advance and drizzled with a little oil just before serving.

# Olive oil buns

*It has often been said that nothing compares to the smell of fresh bread taken straight out of the oven. It is the scent that invites, creating the feeling of homeliness that enslaves all-comers. I always rotate between sourdoughs and fresh olive oil buns, depending on what the occasion calls for. These buns are amongst the most universal in terms of use and perfect for sharing at the dinner table or during a tapas evening.*

*Time* | 90 mins     *Servings* | 8

400 g/14 oz/2⅔ cups all-purpose
  flour
½ tsp salt
2 tsp instant yeast
1½ tbsp sugar
250 ml/1 cup warm water
1 egg, beaten
3 tbsp olive oil

**For egg wash and topping:**
1 egg
1 tbsp water
some fresh rosemary
coarse salt

In a large bowl, whisk the flour, sugar, salt and yeast.

Using a spatula, stir the water, the beaten egg and the oil into the flour until a dough has formed.

Scrape the dough onto a clean, lightly floured surface and knead - scooping, slapping and turning the dough until smooth and elastic (a mixer with a dough hook will work well here too; the dough should be kneaded until it no longer sticks to the sides of the bowl).

Depending on the flour you are using, you may need to add more along the way but don't add too much or the buns will turn out tough. It will take about 8 minutes of kneading for the dough to become nicely elastic.

Shape the dough into a ball and return it to the bowl. Cover the bowl with plastic wrap and allow it to rise in a warm place for at least 1 hour until it has doubled in bulk.

Divide the dough up into 12 parts, shape these into balls and arrange in a greased 20 cm/8-inch baking tin or on a baking tray. Cover with a towel and set aside for at least another hour.

Preheat the oven to 200°C/400°F with a rack in the center.

Beat the egg with the water and brush the mix on top of the buns. Sprinkle with fresh rosemary and coarse salt. Bake for about 15 minutes until golden brown.

◂▴▸

*Tip* | To make sweet buns, top with generous amounts of sugar and cinnamon.

# Fried eggplant with tomato jam

I harbor an extreme affection for the marriage of eggplant and tomatoes and am always on the lookout for new ways to serve them. Fortunately, the possibilities of combining them are apparently endless. My husband, and greatest critic, once told me that this dish was one of the best things I ever came up with, even though it is one of the simplest ones too. Fried eggplant is both crisp and soft, and the sweet tomato jam not only binds it all together, it also makes it easy to spread on toast.

Time | 45 mins    Servings | 4

1 large eggplant or 2 medium ones
100 g/⅔ cup flour
500 ml/2 cups vegetable oil

## Tomato - shallot jam
7 medium tomatoes
2 tbsp olive oil
6 shallots, peeled, halved and sliced
pinch of chili flakes
3 tsp sugar
salt and freshly ground pepper'
2 tsp chopped parsley

## Tomato salad
2 fresh tomatoes, deseeded and diced
1 tbsp balsamic vinegar
1 tbsp extra virgin olive oil
salt and freshly ground black pepper

Start with tomato - shallot jam. Cut a shallow X into the bottom of each tomato and dip them into boiling water for 30 seconds. Run under cold water and peel, deseed and then dice.

Heat the oil in a deep saucepan and fry the shallots on low heat for 10-15 minutes until they have caramelized slightly.

Tip in the tomatoes, chili, and sugar, and season with salt and pepper. Stir from time to time and let it all simmer for about 20 minutes. Taste and adjust seasoning if needed. Stir in the fresh parsley just before serving.

Slice the eggplants into rounds, coat them in flour and fry until golden brown on both sides. Do not overcrowd the pan, as this will reduce the cooking temperature and the eggplants will soak up too much oil. Once fried, transfer them onto a paper towel to absorb any excess oil.

Toss the diced tomato with the oil and vinegar, and season with salt and pepper.

Served the fried eggplant with tomato jam and fresh tomato salad.

Tip | You can make eggplant fries in the very same manner by slicing the eggplant into large sticks. The inner part will melt while the outside will be nice and crisp, making this an excellent accompaniment for summery dishes, such as chicken with romesco sauce (see page 173)

ADAM DE CRAPPONNE
INGENIEVR
NÉ·A·SALON·EN·MDXX
MORT·EN·MDLXXVI

DIX·HVIT·COMMVNES
DES·BOVCHES·DV·RH
AVLDOIVENT·LA·FERT
DE·LEVR·TERRITO

CE·MONVMENT·A·ÉTÉ·ÉRIGÉ
EN·MDCCCLIV
M·DE·CRÈVECŒUR·ÉTANT
PRÉFET·DE·CE·DÉPARTEMENT
ET·M·FIDÈLE·RAYNAUD·MAIRE
DE·SALON·AVEC·LE·CONCOVRS
DES·COMMVNES·CI·APRÈS

SALON·LANÇON·CORNILLON
MARSEILLE·ARLES·CHARLEVAL
MIRAMAS·PÉLISSANNE
LA·ROQVE·D'ANTHÉRON·SÉNAS
FOS·GIGES·GRANS·MÉTEFUIL
STES·MARIES·MARTIGVES
ANNE·LA·CIOTAT·MALLEMORT
ORGON·TARASCON·FEIPIN

# Roasted bell peppers à la Provençal

I can't remember ever visiting Provence without indulging in at least one dish of roasted bell peppers. My mother-in-law is a master of the art and they are almost always the first thing I make upon returning home. I suppose the sweet and herby notes help ease my nostalgia, whisking me as they do directly back to sunny gardens and everlasting aperitifs. This is without doubt my favorite way to enjoy bell peppers. It is one of the dishes that seriously benefits from a prolonged stay in the fridge, and though it is perfectly good after a few hours, allowing the flavors to mature for a few days makes it even better.

Time | 35 mins     Servings | 4

5-8 bell peppers, fresh
5-6 tbsp extra virgin olive oil
a handful of fresh basil, chopped
2 tbsp parsley, chopped
1 small garlic clove, finely chopped
salt and freshly ground pepper

Turn the oven grill on.

Halve the bell peppers, core and place them cut-side down on a tray lined with aluminum foil. Rub the skins with a little olive oil and place under the hot grill until the skins start to blacken. This will take about 20 minutes. Transfer the peppers to a bowl, cover with plastic wrap, and leave to cool. This will loosen the skins, but don't leave the peppers any longer than 15 minutes before peeling off the skins and patting them dry.

Toss the basil with a few tablespoons of olive oil, parsley and garlic, and mix well with the roasted peppers. Season generously with salt and pepper and leave to marinate for at least a few hours in the fridge. Serve with bread.

◄▲►

Tip | One word of advice - using good quality extra virgin olive oil is extremely important in this dish; the better the oil, the better the result.

# Chickpea cakes

The Mediterranean is a marvelous melting pot of a myriad of different cultures. In every nook and cranny of the region you will find some hidden local specialty that the locals invariably swear is unique to their town or village. When traveling through the south of France you might come across panisse – a chickpea flour cake fried to golden perfection. Some say this treat, usually served as an appetizer, is undeniably one of the most delicious specialties of the region and an integral part of street food culture in Southern France. Further afield, in Sicily, you will encounter panelle, often called the quintessential street food of Palermo and which is equally popular in the rest of Sicily. In the same fashion as panisse, panelle is a fried chickpea cake of almost identical constituency and, in my experience, taste. I have also heard rumors of similar fried chickpea concoctions existing in Tunisia, too. Regardless of whatever name you give them, chickpea cakes are wonderful as an appetizer, especially when sliced into sticks, which tricks you into thinking that a plate of tempting French fries is waiting just for you on the table only for it to deliver an unexpected and wonderful surprise upon tasting. I like serving these beauties with cheesy tomato sauce, though they are pretty spectacular on their own as well.

Time | 40 mins    Servings | 4

140 g/5 oz chickpea flour
750 ml/3 cups water
1-2 tbsp olive oil for frying
salt and freshly ground pepper
herby tomato sauce (see page 276)
25g/¼ cup grated parmigiano
  reggiano

Line a small baking tin with plastic wrap.
Take a saucepan and slowly stir the water into the chickpea flour, making sure there are no lumps, and place on a medium heat. Stir for the entire cooking time of 7-10 minutes, then pour into the lined 15 x 15 cm/6 x 6 inch tin and smoothen out the surface. Let it cool for 15 minutes and then slice into fingers.
Heat the olive oil in a nonstick frying pan and fry the chickpea cakes on all sides until golden brown. Transfer onto a paper towel and sprinkle with salt and pepper.
Stir the grated cheese into the tomato sauce and serve along the warm or room temperature chickpea cakes.

# Vin d'orange

Vin d'orange (orange wine) from Provence is a sort of sweet liquor traditionally made from Seville oranges or "bitter oranges", but as they are quite difficult to procure any oranges will do. It's excellent when enjoyed pure as an aperitif or with a dessert, or for a fancy version you can mix some vin d'orange with champagne and have an orange-tasting bubbly cocktail. It takes at least a month to infuse, and the taste will continue to mature when bottled and will also vary depending on how soon you consume it. On a precautionary note, although called an orange wine, this humble drink is much stronger than any wine I have ever previously encountered. So, if you're tempted to have as many glasses of this as you would normally do with a regular wine, then your evening may turn out somewhat shorter than expected.

Time | 10 mins     Servings | 4-6

8 oranges, sliced
1 lemon, sliced
500 g/2½ cups sugar
500 ml/2 cups vodka, 40% alcohol
3 bottles white wine, 750 ml/3 cups each
1 vanilla pod, cut in half

In a glass jar, layer the oranges and lemon and sprinkle with sugar, pour over the vodka and wine, add the vanilla pod and cover tightly. Place in the fridge or in a cool cupboard for about 40 days. Give it a good swirl once or twice a week.

After about 40 days, taste to check if you're happy with the sugar content and add more if needed.

When the vin d'orange is ready, pass it through a triple cloth and if it's still cloudy through a coffee filter. Pour into several bottles, seal and allow to mature for another month or two before serving.

Sealing the bottles: you can use any size or type of bottle you like. If the bottles can be sealed with a cork then this wine can be kept in a cool place for a few years.

When using resealable bottles, it will keep for up to a year in a fridge or a very cool basement.

# Arancini

*A ferry leaves Villa San Giovanni in the tip of southern Italy, bound for Messina. It is crowded with travelers pushing their way to the only food stand on the ship. Behind the counter, hands move swiftly as hefty-looking balls are handed out rapidly, one after another. They still carry the scent of the deep-fat fryer, but the crumbly outside is very inviting. Hidden beneath the crust is a scrumptious surprise: a generous layer of saffron risotto surrounding a rich and luscious meat ragu, and each bite seems to taste better than the previous one. You've just been introduced to arancini, also known as "little oranges", one of Sicily's most popular street snacks and one that boasts an endless variety of rich meat and creamy cheese fillings. I make big batches of arancini with mozzarella every time I am expecting a crowd, and when served with a chilled glass of prosecco they make an outstanding starter.*

Time | 2 hours     Servings | 6-8

**Saffron risotto**

*1 tbsp olive oil*
*30 g/2 tbsp butter*
*1 shallot, very finely chopped*
*1 garlic glove, crushed*
*200 g/7 oz Arborio rice*
*120 ml/½ cup white wine*
*750 ml/3 cups vegetable stock, kept simmering*
*pinch of saffron, crushed*
*salt and freshly ground pepper*
*25g/¼ cup finely grated parmigiano reggiano*

**For the arancini**

*20-30 bocconcini or pieces of mozzarella*
*2 eggs*
*salt and freshly ground pepper*
*250 g/9 oz breadcrumbs*
*500 ml/2 cups vegetable oil*
*herby tomato sauce (see page 276)*

To make the risotto, heat the oil with the butter in a frying pan and gently sauté the chopped shallot and garlic until softened. Add the rice and fry for another minute, stirring all the time. Pour in the wine and cook until it has been completely absorbed, then stir in the stock, a few ladles at a time, until the rice is cooked. This will take about 20 minutes and you may not need all of the stock. Halfway through cooking, add the crushed saffron threads.

When the rice is done, remove the garlic and stir in the cheese. Taste and season and allow to cool completely.

Fill a bowl with cold water, dip your hands in it, take a tablespoon of risotto in the palm of your hand, spread it out as evenly as you can, and then place a mozzarella ball in the center and fold the rice around it shaping it into a ball. Repeat until you have used up all the risotto.

Once the arancini are made, prepare your assembly line: beat the eggs lightly with some salt and pepper, and pour the breadcrumbs into a bowl.

Dip each arancini into the eggs, then into the breadcrumbs and onto a clean plate.

Heat the oil in a deep fryer or casserole and fry the arancini in batches until nicely golden brown, then transfer to a paper towel to absorb any excess oil.

Serve the warm arancini with tomato sauce as a hearty starter or in larger quantities as a main course.

### Tip

Arancini require some time to prepare, but they
can also be made and fried in advance or even
the night before and reheated in a hot oven for
a few minutes before serving.

# Salmon with horseradish lime cream

*These are very pretty-looking and delicious canapés that are ideal for serving at the start of a party. They can also be prepared well in advance. Horseradish lime cream is the star ingredient that binds all of the other ingredients together, so do be generous with it. Your guests will love you for it. These canapés can also be turned into a more filling starter by layering all the ingredients in a glass and serving at the dinner table, though in that case I would suggest you use a whole avocado and half a cucumber in the dish too, and serve crusty bread on the side.*

Time | 30 mins     Servings | 4-6

6 slices of white bread or a whole
   baguette
some olive oil for brushing the bread
200 g/7 oz smoked salmon, thinly
   sliced
½ avocado
juice of half a lime
Fresh cilantro, chopped

**Horseradish lime cream**
3 tbsp mayonnaise
2½ tsp horseradish from a jar
1 tbsp freshly squeezed lime juice
zest of 1 lime, finely grated
salt and freshly ground pepper

Preheat the oven to 190°C/375°F.

Use a round cutter about 2.5cm/1 inch wide to cut out approximately 30 bread circles.

Place them on a tray lined with baking paper, brush with oil and bake for about 10 minutes until light golden brown. Set aside to cool.

Dice the avocado into cubes and squeeze some lime over them to prevent discoloring.

Mix all of the ingredients for the horseradish-lime cream, taste and season as required.

When the toasted bread rounds have cooled down, put the salmon on the toast, followed by a generous dollop of cream, and top off with avocado and a sprinkling of chopped cilantro.

# Chicory canapés

Chicory or Belgian endive leaves can be filled with just about anything to make cute nibbles for a party. I have a preference for Gorgonzola, walnuts, avocado and walnut vinaigrette, but adding figs, cherry tomatoes and other cheeses will work great too.

Time | 20 mins     Servings | 4

2 chicories (Belgian endives)
1 avocado, diced
100 g/3½ oz Gorgonzola cheese, diced
a handful of walnuts

**Walnut vinaigrette**
1 tsp Dijon mustard
2 tbsp white wine vinegar
salt and freshly ground pepper
3 tbsp olive oil
2 tbsp walnut oil

Separate the chicory leaves and dip them into ice cold water for a few minutes to make them more crispy.
Pat dry and transfer onto a plate.
Scatter the avocado, cheese and walnuts onto each leaf.
Whisk the mustard with the vinegar, season with salt and pepper and, while whisking, slowly add both oils.
Spoon the dressing over the chicory cups and serve.

# Lime prosecco punch

This is a very refreshing punch that will fit any season and is the perfect drink for kicking off an evening.

Time | 15 mins     Servings | 6

4 tbsp Grand Marnier
2 limes, juice and zest
2-3 tbsp sugar syrup
1 bottle of Prosecco, chilled

Mix all of the ingredients together, taste, and add more lime or syrup if required before serving.

Tip | A simple syrup is nothing more than 1 part water and 2 parts sugar that you allow to simmer until all of the sugar has dissolved. It can be stored in an airtight container for later use in cocktails.

# Mulled cider

*I always begin making hot cider when the last leaves are falling off the trees and Christmas is just around the corner. It has a way of filling the home with a most wonderful aroma that invites you to cozy up on the sofa with a warm blanket and a good book to nourish the soul.*

Time | 15 mins     Servings | 8

1 liter/4 cups cider
2 tbsp light brown sugar
1 orange, sliced
1 cinnamon stick
1 vanilla pod, halved

Add all of the ingredients to a saucepan and bring to the boil. Reduce to a simmer and continue to cook for another 7-10 minutes before serving. Mulled cider can also be prepared in advance and reheated.

# Sweet potato hummus

*Hummus has become a regular at every party we throw, but this version (which is so different to the classic version that it can be barely be called hummus at all) is by far the best. The bright orange color always sparks curiosity and the taste is most unexpected: rich and creamy, and both sweet and lightly sour and, most importantly, absolutely delicious.*

**Time** | 35 mins    **Servings** | 6

2 large sweet potatoes, peeled, quartered and sliced
4-8 tbsp extra virgin olive oil
salt and freshly ground pepper
5-7 tbsp water
2-3 tbsp lemon juice
3 tbsp tahini
1 tbsp za'atar

Preheat the oven to 220°C/430°F.

Line a baking tray with baking paper

Toss the potatoes with 4 tablespoons of oil, season with salt and pepper, and roast for 20-30 minutes.

Once out of the oven, transfer to a food processor, add the water, lemon juice and tahini, and pulse until you have a smooth paste. Start with a small amount of the added ingredients first and add more lemon juice, tahini, water and oil as needed.

Pour into a bowl, sprinkle with za'atar and drizzle with a little olive oil and serve.

# Balsamic shallot relish

*It should be noted that cheese is essential in many ways and should never be disregarded. It has a knack of starting a conversation - people are always pointing out their favorites - and I can hardly imagine a gathering where a generous platter of cheese would not be served just before the sweets hit the table. This platter, rather than just a simple plate, loaded with cheeses of various characters and temperaments, should be followed by a generous stack of salad and almost certainly a couple of fresh baguettes. With the cheese making its way around the table, a couple of jams or relishes should also be forced to wait impatiently for their moment of fame when the creamy constituency of a cheese calls for their help.*

Time | 30 mins       Servings | 4

5 large shallots (or 8 small ones), halved and thinly sliced
1 tbsp olive oil
1 sprig of thyme (optional)
1 sprig of rosemary (optional)
pinch of salt
7 tbsp balsamic vinegar
2 tbsp brown sugar
200 g/7 oz blue cheese (e.g. gorgonzola)
1 baguette, sliced

Heat the oil in a nonstick frying pan and sauté the shallots for about 5-10 minutes with the thyme and rosemary.

Season with salt, pour in the balsamic vinegar and continue cooking until the vinegar is almost gone. This will take about 10-15 minutes, maybe a bit more.

Add the sugar, turn up the heat and leave to bubble a bit until all the sugar has dissolved; it will start caramelizing immediately, so a few more minutes on the heat will probably be enough.

Check the consistency. If it's too thick it will be difficult to spread. In that case add a few more drops of balsamic vinegar and cook for a little longer before removing from the heat.

You can either serve it directly or allow it to cool down and store it in an airtight container for a few days in the fridge. Before serving, heat for a couple of minutes in the oven. Serve with cheese and bread.

# Walnut salad

Time | 5 mins    Servings | 4

200 g/7 oz of mixed salad leaves
a handful of walnuts

**Vinaigrette**
1 tbsp Dijon mustard
2 tbsp red wine vinegar
salt and freshly ground pepper
3 tbsp extra virgin olive oil
2 tbsp walnut oil

Whisk the mustard with the vinegar, season with salt and pepper, and slowly add both oils until the vinaigrette is completely homogenous. Toss the salad with the walnuts and serve the vinaigrette on the side.

# Red wine onion jam

Time | 40 mins    Servings | 4-6

4 large onions, halved and thinly
    sliced
2 tbsp extra virgin olive oil
1 tbsp brown sugar
2 tbsp balsamic vinegar
1 sprig of rosemary
500 ml/2 cups red wine
salt and freshly ground pepper

Heat the oil in a heavy based frying pan and fry the onions on a medium-high heat for 10-15 minutes until they start to caramelize; then add the sugar. Stir in 1 tbsp of balsamic vinegar and allow it to bubble away for a while before adding the rosemary.

Next you can either pour in all the wine at once and slowly reduce it until it has achieved a jam-like consistency or, if you want to give more flavor to the jam, add the wine in 3-4 batches, allowing each batch to reduce and caramelize on the bottom before adding the next one. This will give the jam a deeper flavor.

During the last 5 minutes of cooking, stir in the remaining tablespoon of balsamic vinegar. Season with salt and freshly ground pepper.

# Light meals

*I can barely recall any occasion, while in the vicinity of the Mediterranean, that could be described as particularly 'light', for food is never a swift affair there nor perhaps should it be. Lunch is meant to provide a little oasis in the middle of the day and to supply one with enough fuel to keep going until it is time to dine. I love light meals and this chapter is dedicated to quick lunches or lovely starters to a larger meal.*

# Smoked eggplant with mozzarella

I think it is almost magical how the humble eggplant transforms itself under blistering heat and slowly attains a distinctive smokiness. Love is maybe even too weak a word to describe how I feel about smoked eggplant. I unconditionally and unapologetically adore it. If it weren't for the fact that making it too frequently would result in my kitchen acquiring the peculiar and lingering scent of a smokehouse, I am pretty certain it would be on the menu every day. This is a very simple version, with the mozzarella squeezed between the eggplant and hot roasted tomatoes. A melt-in-your-mouth delight and simplicity at its very best.

Time | 1 hour     Servings | 4

4 eggplants
250 g/9 oz cherry tomatoes, halved
6 garlic cloves, halved
3-5 tbsp extra virgin olive oil
salt and freshly ground pepper
1-2 tbsp balsamic vinegar
1 large buffalo mozzarella
4 slices of toasted bread
fresh basil leaves

Turn the oven grill on.

Using the tip of a knife, poke each eggplant in a few spots, arrange on a tray lined with aluminum foil, and place under the grill for about 45 minutes. They are done when the skin is blackened and crispy and a strong smoky aroma greets you when you open the door of the oven.

While the eggplants are grilling away, take a second tray and quickly toss in the tomato halves along with the garlic and oil, season with salt and pepper and place under the eggplant tray. They will roast lightly.

Once the eggplants are done, take them out of the oven, turn the oven to 200°C/400°F and continue to roast the cherry tomatoes. In the meantime, remove the pulp from the roasted eggplants and transfer to a sieve for about 10 minutes to drain a little. Then mix gently with balsamic vinegar and season with salt and pepper.

Divide the eggplant over the toasted bread, tear up some mozzarella and place it on top, and finish with the roasted tomatoes, the basil leaves and the juices from the roasted tomatoes.

◀▲▶

A must-try | A bit of tahini strengthens the flavor of eggplants, making baba ghanoush - an irresistible treat. To make this, roast the eggplants according to the recipe above and drain off any excess liquid completely before mixing together with a few tablespoons of tahini, chopped parsley, lemon juice, the zest of 1 lemon and about 5 tbsp of extra virgin olive oil. Don't forget to season with salt and pepper and to enjoy shamelessly.

# Couscous salad

*I really do not know what I would do without couscous. Most likely I would never get to taste my favorite salad, which is so easy to make and so addictive that in summer months, when tomatoes are at their best, it makes an appearance on our table at least twice a week and is a lifesaver when you need to feed a crowd. When preparing couscous salads like this one, it is worth keeping in mind that couscous, although smashingly delicious in the right context, does not by itself carry much flavor and relies on a cast of supporting characters to unleash its potential. Herbs and stock (preferably chicken) play key roles en route to a delicious couscous dish, as does sumac, helping to lift everything to a new level of deliciousness.*

Time | 30 mins     Servings | 4

250 ml/1 cup chicken stock
120 g/4 oz/⅔ cup couscous
1 small eggplant, sliced
3-4 tbsp extra virgin olive oil
1 avocado, diced
2 tomatoes, diced
1 cucumber, deseeded and diced
a bunch of parsley, chopped
a large bunch of cilantro, chopped
1 lemon, juice and grated zest
salt and freshly ground pepper
1 tbsp sumac

**Toasted almonds**
80 g/3 oz almonds
1 tbsp olive oil

Boil the stock and pour over the couscous, cover with plastic wrap and leave to cook for 10 minutes. Using your fingertips, break up any lumps that may have formed so as to ensure a lighter texture in the salad.

Heat a griddle pan until very hot. Brush the eggplant with olive oil, and grill on both sides for a few minutes. Add to the couscous along with the other vegetables and herbs.

Mix well, add the olive oil, add lemon juice and zest, and season with salt, sumac and pepper. Let it stand for at least 20 minutes. This will allow the flavor to develop.

In the meantime, heat the oil and fry the almonds on a medium heat for 4-5 minutes, shaking frequently. Season with salt and pepper, shake well to coat and pour onto a paper towel to drain off any excess oil. Serve on top of the couscous salad.

# Tomato carpaccio

*I have had an inexhaustible love affair with tomatoes for as long as I can remember. My grandmother used to grow lots of them, especially coeur de boeuf, which in my humble opinion are the crème de la crème of tomato society. Served with homemade sour cream and black rye bread they were an all-time favorite, until a trip to Pamplona in Spain some years ago, however, when I was given my first taste of something else. In all truth, until it was right under my nose I was certain beef carpaccios were on the menu. I was mistaken, but the paper-thin tomato slices soaked in citrus juice and covered with a blanket of herbs and cheese were as good-looking as their taste was revelatory. The subtle flavor was puzzling and so utterly delicious that it became a frequent guest in our house, particularly at swift lunches or when served on a big platter as a starter during a summer dinner party. I suspect this dish will more than please fellow tomato lovers.*

Time | 20 mins     Servings | 4

5 tomatoes
juice of half a lemon
salt and freshly ground pepper
8 basil leaves, finely chopped
1 tbsp parsley, finely chopped
extra virgin olive oil for drizzling
50-70 g/½ cup grated parmigiano
  reggiano or manchego

Slice the tomatoes as thinly as you possibly can. Arrange on two serving plates, squeeze plenty of lemon juice on top, and leave for 10-15 minutes to marinate.

Before serving, season well with salt and pepper, sprinkle the finely chopped herbs on top, drizzle with oil, and top off with lots of grated cheese.

# Octopus salad

If my husband had his way we would be eating octopus every single day of the week. Though come to think of it, that would probably be my wish too. Cooked to perfection using the most humble of ingredients, this dish is both peculiar (in the best sense of the word) and utterly delicious, and one that requires no fancy additions. Octopus can be found prepared this way at every corner restaurant all across the south of Italy, much to my and my husband's delight. Do not be intimidated by the legs of an octopus; they may seem difficult to handle at first but always turn out to be quite easy. The key to a delicious octopus dish is a well-tenderized octopus. You can either buy it already tenderized or try a couple of simple ways of doing it yourself at home.

Time | 55 mins    Servings | 2-4

600 g/21 oz octopus (legs only)
1 lemon, zest and juice
1½ tbsp red wine vinegar
5 tbsp extra virgin olive oil
salt and freshly ground pepper
fresh parsley, chopped
lemon zest, optional

Bring a large pot of salted water to the boil, tip in the octopus and cook for 20-25 minutes on a medium-high heat until tender when pierced with a fork. Let it rest for another 20 minutes in the water with the heat turned off. Drain and slice.

Mix the lemon juice, zest, vinegar and olive oil together and season with salt and pepper. Toss with the sliced octopus and fresh parsley, taste, sprinkle the lemon zest on top and serve.

Tip | If you cannot get your hands on octopus that has already been tenderized, the easiest way is to freeze it for 1-2 days and let it thaw for another day in the fridge. Otherwise, smashing the octopus continuously for a few minutes into the kitchen counter will work too (and get rid of any pent-up anger), but freezing is a less messy procedure.

# Puy lentil, feta and tomato salad

*I have often made this salad for people who insist that they are not fond of lentils and it has never failed to bring about a change of heart. A very tangy and herby vinaigrette is my secret ingredient here, which when paired with meaty lentils, creamy cheese and fresh tomatoes results in an unexpected plate full of surprising flavors.*

Time | 30 mins    Servings | 2-4

150 g/5½ oz/⅔ cup Puy lentils
1 1/4 cups vegetable stock
1 eggplant, sliced lengthways
250 g/9 oz cherry tomatoes, halved
100 g/3½ oz feta cheese

**Balsamic cilantro vinaigrette**
1 garlic clove
pinch of chili flakes
a handful of basil leaves, chopped
4 tbsp good quality balsamic vinegar
salt and freshly ground pepper
4 tbsp extra virgin olive oil
a handful of cilantro, chopped

Bring the stock to the boil, add the lentils and cook for 15-20 minutes. When ready, drain and set aside.

Chargrill the eggplant for a few minutes on each side. Leave to cool for a few minutes, and then chop. Toss together with the lentils, tomatoes and feta cheese.

Using a mortar and pestle, grind together the garlic, dried chili and half of the basil leaves until you have a smooth paste. Add the balsamic vinegar and oil and continue to stir until well combined. Finish with cilantro and the rest of the basil. Serve the salad either warm or cold with a dash of vinaigrette.

# Roasted asparagus and avocado salad

*I am one of those enthusiasts who eagerly wait for springtime when fresh local asparagus starts popping up everywhere and every restaurant tries to come up with new ways of preparing this incredibly versatile vegetable. Though the possibilities are endless, I don't think there is anything better than pure, grilled asparagus, unless there are some roasted tomatoes involved. Roasting not only concentrates the flavor of tomatoes; it also creates the most wonderful and aromatic vinaigrette that can be used directly on any salad or pasta, or spread on a generous slice of toasted ciabatta.*

Time | 2 hours    Servings | 2-4

300 g/10½ oz cherry tomatoes, halved
6 garlic cloves, halved
a few sprigs of fresh rosemary
a few sprigs of fresh thyme
5 tablespoons extra virgin olive oil
2 tbsp balsamic vinegar
salt and freshly ground pepper
30 g/1 oz pine nuts
1 bunch of asparagus, woody ends removed
1 avocado
parmigiano reggiano shavings
handful of fresh basil leaves

Preheat the oven to 160°C/320°F.

Place the cherry tomatoes on a baking tray, scatter over the garlic, thyme and rosemary, drizzle with olive oil and balsamic, season with salt and pepper, and leave to roast for about an hour to an hour and a half. Halfway through roasting, scatter the pine nuts on top.

Place the asparagus on a plate, drizzle with olive oil, season with salt and pepper, and leave to marinate for anything from 30 minutes up to 2 hours.

15 minutes before serving, turn your oven grill to its highest setting and grill the asparagus for about 10 minutes. If they are very thick it may take 15 minutes.

Slice the avocado and arrange on a serving platter, add the grilled asparagus and top off with the roasted tomatoes and their juices. Finish off with parmigiano reggiano shavings and the basil leaves and serve.

# Spicy beans

*This is a wonderful vegetarian dish, both spicy and flavorsome and quite perfect for lunch or dinner, especially when the weather gets a little less friendly. Depending on the season, the sauce can be made with either fresh or tinned tomatoes, though fresh tomato sauce is always that little bit better.*

**Time** | 1 hour (start the day before)     **Servings** | 2 - 4

200 g/7 oz dried gigantes or dried
   butter beans or simple white beans
1 tbsp olive oil
2 shallots, chopped
4 garlic cloves, chopped
1-2 tsp harissa
1 tsp cumin powder
1 tsp sugar
300 g/10½ oz cherry tomatoes,
   halved, or 400 g/14 oz tinned
   tomatoes
3 tbsp chopped parsley
salt
feta (optional)

Soak the beans overnight, then rinse, cover with 1½ liters of cold water, bring to the boil and simmer for about 45 minutes until they are tender. Drain.

While the beans are simmering, heat the oil in a pan and fry the shallots until they soften. Stir in the garlic, harissa and cumin and fry for one more minute. Finally, add the sugar, tomatoes and parsley, season with salt, and leave to simmer for about 10 minutes.

Add the drained beans and simmer for another 10-15 minutes. If the sauce gets too dry add a little water.

Serve with feta and lots of fresh bread.

# Avocado with smoky lentils

*I adore the taste of Spanish smoked paprika, which tastes rather harsh when eaten raw but under a little heat it can give an addictive smoky aroma to your dishes. This is my 'to-go' dish for both lunch and dinner when I don't even feel like stepping into the kitchen (it happens to all of us) but still have a craving for something special.*

Time | 20 mins    Servings | 4

140 g/5 oz/⅔ cup Puy lentils
1 tbsp extra virgin olive oil
1 onion, halved and sliced
4 garlic cloves, chopped
pinch of chili flakes
1 tsp smoked paprika
400 g/14 oz canned tomatoes
½ tsp sugar
salt and freshly ground pepper
2 avocados
2-3 tbsp cilantro, chopped

Add the lentils to 1 liter of boiling water and cook for about 15 minutes. Then drain.

While the lentils are cooking, heat the oil and fry the onion until translucent. Add the garlic, chili flakes and smoked paprika and fry for another minute.

Stir in the tomatoes and sugar and season with salt and pepper. Leave to simmer for 5-10 minutes. Taste and adjust the seasoning.

Tip in the lentils, stir and remove from the heat.

Halve the avocados, core them and top everything off with smoky lentils and chopped cilantro.

# Pearl barley and roasted carrot salad

*I appreciate barley almost just as much as couscous for being a perfect medium for both taste and texture. It's rather bland on its own, so barley begs for bold flavors, fresh herbs and even a spicy kick now and then. And when all of these elements are in place it makes for a very lovely meal.*

Time | 55 mins     Servings | 2

100 g/3½ oz pearl barley
8 carrots, peeled and halved
2 tbsp extra virgin olive oil
1-2 tsp harissa
1 tsp cumin powder
3 garlic cloves, halved, skins on
2 tbsp orange juice
salt
30 g/1 oz almonds, roughly chopped
30 g/1 oz pistachios, roughly chopped
1 avocado
½ pomegranate seeds
2 tbsp parsley, chopped
2 tbsp coriander, chopped
1 tsp sumac
zest of 1 orange
1 lime, zest and juice
feta cheese (optional)

Cook the barley according to the instructions on the package, drain and allow to cool a little.

Preheat the oven to 200°C/400°F.

Peel and halve the carrots and place on a tray lined with baking paper.

Whisk the oil with the harissa and 2 tbsp orange juice, stir in the cumin and then coat the carrots, sprinkle with salt and toss in the garlic halves. Roast everything in the oven for 15-20 minutes. For the last 5 minutes, scatter the almonds and pistachios on top.

Slice the avocado and mix with the barley, pomegranate seeds, chopped parsley and coriander. Season with salt, sumac, orange zest and lime zest, and add some lime juice to taste.

Top off with the juices from the roasted carrots, the nuts and the feta cheese.

# Scallops with chestnuts and roasted Jerusalem artichokes

*Scallops are so incredibly flavorsome on their own that most of the time we eat them simply sautéed in butter. However, on occasions when a slightly larger meal is called for, roasted Jerusalem artichokes and chestnuts go perfectly with these delicious treasures of the sea.*

Time | 40 mins     Servings | 2

3 Jerusalem artichokes, halved

1-2 tablespoons extra virgin olive oil

salt and freshly ground pepper

a good handful of green beans, ends trimmed

30 g/2 tbsp butter

6 scallops

1 shallot, finely diced

3 slices pancetta, chopped

6 roasted chestnuts, sliced

4 tbsp red wine vinegar,

1 tbsp parsley, chopped

lemon zest to garnish

Preheat the oven to 200°C/400°F.

Arrange the Jerusalem artichoke halves on a tray, drizzle with a little oil, season with salt and pepper, and roast for 25-35 minutes until tender.

Cook the beans for 3 minutes in boiling salted water, drain, and dip into ice-cold water to preserve their color. Drain and set aside.

Just before serving, heat a non-stick frying pan until very hot, add the butter, season the scallops with salt and pepper, and fry for about 1-1½ minutes on each side. Remove the scallops from the pan and keep warm. Immediately tip in the shallot and pancetta and fry for a few minutes. Add the chestnuts and the beans, toss around a little, and deglaze the pan with red wine vinegar and remove from the heat.

Serve the scallops with the roasted Jerusalem artichokes, chestnuts, beans and warm vinaigrette. Finish off with a sprinkling of parsley and lemon zest

# Smoked mackerel salad

*Mackerel is an oily fish that always asks for something fresh on the side. When smoked it always works impeccably in salads, with oranges and avocados, and it can be both a lovely starter and, in larger quantities, a filling meal.*

*Time* | 30 mins    *Servings* | 2-4

2 oranges
5-6 medium-sized potatoes, peeled and
    cut into equal chunks
2 avocados
leaves of 2 heads of little gem lettuce
2 smoked mackerel fillets, broken into
    pieces

**Vinaigrette**
6 tbsp fresh orange juice
2 tsp whole grain mustard
2 tbsp red wine vinegar
salt and freshly ground pepper
3 tbsp extra virgin olive oil

To segment the oranges, first slice off the top and bottom. Then place each orange on a chopping board, hold down firmly, and cut the skin off the sides to reveal the segments. Make an incision on both sides of each segment and they will fall out. Do so with a bowl placed under the orange so that you can gather all the juices, which you can then use to make the vinaigrette.

For the vinaigrette, whisk the orange juice, mustard and vinegar together and season with salt and pepper. Stir in the oil quite vigorously until you have a homogenous sauce.

Boil the potatoes in salted water. When ready, drain and return the saucepan to the heat for a few seconds to allow any leftover moisture to evaporate. Coat the potatoes in a few tablespoons of vinaigrette so that they can absorb all the flavors.

Peel, pit and slice the avocado.

To serve, arrange a few lettuce leaves on the plates and add the potatoes, orange segments and avocados. Break the smoked mackerel on top and spoon over some extra vinaigrette.

*Tip* | The best way to taste the vinaigrette is with a green salad leaf. Be sure that the vinaigrette is well mixed before doing so, otherwise you'll taste nothing but the oil floating on top.

# Beet, spinach and goat's cheese salad

*There was a time when my tastes buds were a little less adventurous and the very idea of a dish that involved beets would have me running for the hills. I suppose this could best be described as a love/hate relationship without much love involved and perhaps the lingering memory of sampling badly prepared beets in the past. The beet is a bit of a funky vegetable whose flavor can change dramatically, depending on how it is handled. Boiled it looses all its delicacy, as the precious flavor becomes diluted; roasting, on the other hand, concentrates and brings out its pleasant sweetness. But you get the best results, in my humble opinion, when you cover it with plenty of balsamic vinegar and let time work its magic. This simple and uncomplicated process transforms beets into something utterly delicious, and when paired with blood oranges and creamy goat's cheese it makes a perfect meal while awaiting the gifts of spring.*

*Time* | 20 mins (start the day before)     *Servings* | 2

2 large beets

4 tbsp balsamic vinegar

2 blood oranges, segmented

a few handfuls of lollo rosso lettuce
   leaves (or any other variety)

a handful of spinach leaves

150 g/5½ oz goat's cheese

**Dressing**

a handful of hazelnuts

2 tsp Dijon mustard

1 tbsp balsamic vinegar

Zest of 2 blood oranges

2 tbsp blood orange juice (from
   segmenting)

1 tsp honey

salt and freshly ground pepper

2 tbsp extra virgin olive oil

2 tsp sumac

The day before: peel and slice the beet as thinly as possible, preferably using a mandolin.

Place in a shallow bowl, pour over 4 tablespoons of balsamic vinegar, cover and leave to marinate in the fridge overnight.

Before serving, take the beets out of the fridge, drain, and let them come up to room temperature.

Slice off the top and bottom parts of the blood oranges and carefully slice off the rest of the skin with a knife, holding the blood orange firmly on the chopping board. Make careful incisions on both sides of the segments and release them and their juices into a bowl. Once done, give the oranges a good squeeze to get all the juice out.

Reserve 2 tablespoons of juice for the dressing and combine the lettuce and spinach leaves and dress them with the rest of the juice.

For the dressing, toast the hazelnuts in a dry pan for a few minutes, shaking frequently, then chop/crush them roughly.

Whisk together the mustard, vinegar, zest, blood orange juice and honey. Season with salt and pepper, and then stir in the olive oil and hazelnuts.

Arrange the beets on a plate by starting with circles of beets on the outer edge and then moving in gradually to the center.

Scatter the orange segments and pieces of goat's cheese on top, spoon over some hazelnut vinaigrette and sprinkle with sumac. Serve with the salad and crusty bread.

# Cauliflower couscous with oozy egg yolk

Over the years cauliflower has graduated from being the least to one of my most cherished vegetables. I believe that my opinion of cauliflower as a bland and rather uninteresting vegetable was changed forever the moment I tried it after dipping it in a mustardy French vinaigrette in my mother-in-law's kitchen. Like a chameleon, it changes and adapts to its surroundings and the manner in which it is prepared. Roasted and a little croquant it's a wonderful snack with spiced labneh, and it is equally delicious when tossed with a simple balsamic dressing. Maybe even better is when you grind cauliflower in a food processor to produce a couscous-like texture, which is both exciting and different and can even be used raw as an alternative to regular couscous. I cook mine just a little and finish it off with generous amounts of herbs and poached egg.

Time | 30 mins    Servings | 2

1 medium-sized cauliflower, cut into small pieces
2 tbsp olive oil
1 onion, finely diced
3 medium-sized carrots, halved and sliced
a handful of dried apricots, diced
grated zest of 1 orange
grated zest and juice of 1 lemon
1 tbsp sumac
Salt and freshly ground pepper
3 tbsp parsley, chopped
1 tbsp basil leaves, chopped
seeds of ½ pomegranate
2 eggs
2 tbsp white wine vinegar

**Smoky almonds**
1 tbsp olive oil
a small handful of almonds
salt and freshly ground pepper
¼ tsp smoked paprika

Blend the cauliflower in a food processor until it starts to resemble couscous. In a large frying pan, heat the oil and fry the onion until it softens. Once the onion has softened, add the carrots and fry for another few minutes. Stir in the cauliflower and, stirring frequently, fry for another few minutes. Finally, add the zest and apricots and remove from the heat.

Season with sumac and salt and pepper and add the lemon juice according to taste. Stir in the parsley, basil, pomegranates (optional) and set aside until serving.

To poach the eggs, bring a few liters of water to the boil in a large shallow saucepan, stir in the vinegar and reduce the heat to low. The secret is to keep the temperature just a little below boiling, somewhere between 65°C-85°C/150°F-185°F.

Crack each egg into a small bowl and gently slide them into the water. Cook for about 4 minutes and then remove with a slotted spoon onto a paper towel to dry.

For the smoky almonds, take a small saucepan, heat the oil, add the almonds and cook on a medium heat for 4-5 minutes, shaking frequently. Season with salt, pepper and smoked paprika, shake well to coat and pour onto a paper towel to drain off any excess oil. Chop the almonds roughly.

Serve the cauliflower couscous with a poached egg and chopped smoky almonds.

# Crispy squid rings

*This is a dish I keep getting asked to make over and over again, even though it is as simple as dishes come. You might have heard that squid can be tricky to cook, and a few seconds can certainly make all the difference between raw or rubbery fish, but when done right squid is simply delicious and this recipe works every time. The squid rings are both crispy and melt-in-your-mouth delicious and they just beg for a fresh sauce as an accompaniment. In smaller quantities they make a great appetizer and in larger ones a fulfilling meal.*

*Time* | 45 mins     *Servings* | 2 - 4

4 squids, cleaned
120 g/¾ cup flour
2 eggs, beaten with salt and freshly
    ground pepper
200 g/7 oz breadcrumbs
750 ml/3 cups vegetable oil
herby tomato sauce (see page 276)

Slice the squids into rings about 5mm thick. Dip each squid ring into the flour, the egg and finally the breadcrumbs. Repeat with the rest.

Heat the oil in a deep fryer or casserole (test to see if it is hot enough by dropping in a pinch of flour; it should sizzle immediately) and fry the squid rings until they are golden brown. Remove with a slotted spoon and place on a paper towel to absorb any excess oil. You might need to do this in batches so as not to overcrowd the pan, otherwise the temperature of the oil will drop and the squid rings will absorb too much oil.

Serve the fried squid with the herby tomato sauce.

# Grilled apple and goat's cheese salad

*Warm goat's cheese melting between grilled apple slices sprinkled with a refreshing dressing is a wonderful and healthy treat that can be prepared in minutes. It also looks pretty on a plate and is a great addition to dinner parties.*

Time | 30 mins    Servings | 2

a handful of cherry tomatoes, halved

extra virgin olive oil

salt and freshly ground pepper

1 apple (e.g. Gala)

2 small fresh goat's cheeses, sliced
  horizontally

1 avocado

1 head of Romaine lettuce

30 g/1 oz almonds, toasted and
  roughly chopped

**Vinaigrette**

1½ tbsp honey

3 tbsp cider vinegar (or white wine
  vinegar)

½ tsp lemon zest

1 tbsp lemon juice

salt and freshly ground pepper

3 tbsp olive oil

Turn on the oven grill. Place the tomato halves on a baking tray, drizzle with a little olive oil, season with salt and pepper and place under a hot grill for 15-20 minutes.

Make the vinaigrette by whisking together the honey, vinegar, zest and juice. Season and slowly add the olive oil until you have a homogenous dressing. Dip a salad leaf in to taste and add more lemon juice, salt and pepper if required.

Slice the apple, core, and dip the slices in the vinaigrette to coat. Heat a griddle pan until very hot and then quickly chargrill the apple slices on both sides. Set aside.

When the tomatoes are done, take them out of the oven and turn off the grill. Place the goat's cheese on a baking tray and place in the warm oven for a few minutes. Peel the avocado and slice it up.

To serve, arrange the salad leaves on the plates along with the apple slices, goat's cheese, avocado and roasted tomatoes. Sprinkle some almonds on top and spoon over the vinaigrette.

# Pumpkin and cinnamon soup

*As someone who grew up in a place where in winter the temperature can tumble to unacceptable lows, I am firm believer in soups. From the moment when the first frost touches the ground to after it has mercifully vanished, soups are a necessary part of daily life in Lithuania. There is something magical about the aroma of pumpkin roasting in the oven. It gently tickles the nose and entices the taste buds with its delicious promise and this soup does exactly the same: slightly sweet and spicy, filling enough to be served as a main course and most welcome on cold and rainy days.*

Time | 40 mins     Servings | 4

1 small pumpkin or butternut
   squash
2 tbsp extra virgin olive oil
salt and freshly ground pepper
1 onion, peeled and roughly
   chopped
1 medium sized carrot, roughly
   chopped
1 tsp cinnamon
1 tbsp brown sugar
1 tsp ginger, chopped
500 ml/2 cups chicken stock
250 ml/1 cup cream or milk

**Topping**
1 chili, finely chopped
50 g/2 oz pine nuts or cashew
   nuts, toasted
fresh cilantro or parsley, chopped

Preheat the oven to 210°C/410°F.

Slice the pumpkin in pieces and roast for 25-30 minutes with a little olive oil, salt and pepper. You can either peel the pumpkin before roasting or scoop the flesh out with a spoon before adding to the soup.

Heat 1 tbsp of oil in a heavy based frying pan and fry the onion for 5 minutes before adding the chopped carrots and cooking for a few more minutes

Stir in the cinnamon, ginger and sugar and cook for 1 minute, stirring all the time. Add the stock and simmer for another 5 minutes. Finally, add the roasted pumpkin and blend everything together (a hand-held blender will work just fine).

Stir in the cream or milk and season with salt and pepper to taste.

Top with fresh chili, nuts and chopped cilantro.

# Slow-roasted cherry tomato soup

*I am exceptionally fond of using tomatoes in almost everything we eat, but this soup has all the deliciousness of these bursting gems concentrated in a single bowl and is a most comforting treat on a rainy day. It doesn't require much hands-on work, but needs every minute you can give it in the oven. Roasting the tomatoes slowly will bring out their natural sweetness, and anything below the few hours roasting time required won't unleash the full potential of this dish. Patience is a virtue that pays off handsomely every time.*

Time | 2 hours    Servings | 4

1 large onion
1 kg/35 oz cherry tomatoes
8 garlic cloves, skins on
a few sprigs of rosemary
salt and freshly ground pepper
5 tbsp extra virgin olive oil
500 ml/2 cups chicken stock (or
   vegetable stock for vegetarian
   version)
parmigiano reggiano shavings
handful of basil (4-5 leaves per
   portion)

Preheat the oven to 160°C/320°F and line a tray with baking paper.
Peel, halve and thinly slice the onion. Scatter on the tray. Halve the cherry tomatoes and place them cut side up on top of the onion. Halve the garlic cloves (skins still on) and scatter them between the tomatoes. Top off with the rosemary, seasoning and olive oil. Be sure that all the garlic and onions are well covered in oil.
Roast for 2 hours. Once out of the oven, remove the rosemary and peel the garlic. Place the cherry tomatoes in a blender along with the onions, garlic, chicken stock and some of the oil from the baking tray and blend until smooth. Taste and adjust the seasoning; if the soup is too thick add more stock.
Serve with parmigiano shavings and fresh basil on top.

# Chestnut and fennel soup with taleggio toast

*This is one of my trickier soups. Its color is neither bright nor eye-popping, and thus does not create much in the way of anticipation or give away just how delicious it actually is. Caramelizing fennel creates more flavor, as does adding fennel seeds. And the cherry on the cake, so to speak, is the Taleggio toast, which perfectly matches the autumn flavors of the soup.*

Time | 30 mins    Servings | 4

2 tbsp extra virgin olive oil

1 large fennel or 2 small ones, about 300 g/10½ oz

2 shallots

1 tbsp fennel seeds

zest of 1 lemon

300 g/10½ oz roasted chestnuts, roughly chopped

1 1/4 cups chicken or vegetable stock

salt and freshly ground pepper

200 ml/¾ cup milk or cream

2 tbsp parsley, chopped

**To serve**

A few slices of toasted bread

A few slices of Taleggio cheese

Heat a wide casserole dish until very hot; add the oil and fennel and cook, stirring frequently, for about 5 minutes until the fennel starts to caramelize.

Add the shallots and fennel seeds and continue to cook for another minute. Finally, stir in the zest, chestnuts and stock. Season the soup with salt and pepper and cook for another 15-20 minutes. Remove from the heat and leave to cool for a few minutes, then blend in batches and stir in the milk. Return to the heat and allow it to simmer for a while; taste and adjust the seasoning. Stir in the parsley just before serving.

Place the cheese on the toasted bread and melt under the grill for about a minute. Serve the soup hot with the Taleggio toast.

# Hangover soup

*Sounds like an odd one, I know, and this soup probably has about as much in common with Mediterranean flavors as borscht does, but it was one of my favorite dishes as a child so I just had to include it (please do not get any wrong ideas because of its name!). It is a very nourishing soup and one that would be found simmering on the stove in our house in wintertime on an almost daily basis. Its deeply comforting taste, with loads of bacon, is hard to come by these days. The name 'hangover soup' comes from the tradition of serving it on the morning of the second day of a wedding celebration in Lithuania (traditional Lithuanian weddings can last for up to three days) because of its reputedly magical ability to restore even the hardest partygoers to good health. But it is also just a wonderful soup for keeping you warm through cold winter months.*

*Time* | 1 hour    *Servings* | 6-8

100 g/3½ oz bacon, diced
2 small onions, chopped
2 medium-sized carrots, grated
2 tbsp tomato paste
2½ l/10 cups water
500 g/18 oz sauerkraut
2-4 tbsp sugar
salt and freshly ground pepper
Crème fraiche

Heat a heavy based saucepan and gently fry the bacon. When it has released enough fat add the onions and fry for another 5 minutes. Tip in the grated carrots and fry for an additional 3 minutes.

Stir in the tomato paste and coat all the ingredients thoroughly.

Finally, pour in the water, add the sauerkraut and bring to boil. Stir in the sugar (start with 2 tablespoons) and let it all simmer for 30-50 minutes.

Taste; if it is too sour add more sugar or more seasoning, and leave to simmer for another 10 minutes before tasting again. Serve hot with a generous dollop of crème fraiche.

# Snippets of Italy

Italy is without a doubt home to some of the most delicious pasta and risotto concoctions, many of which, I might add, still lie hidden deep in ancient villages perched on mountaintops or in the most humble-looking trattorias. Their variety is endless and with every new trip, even back to familiar territory, I always discover something new and inspiring when it comes to ways of serving them. So if you ever find yourself unable to decide whether to serve risotto or pasta, take the Sicilian way and serve both.

# Basic pasta recipe

*It may seem a little old-fashioned, but I think there is something poetic about making pasta, where flour and eggs come together to form something magical. There are more myths surrounding the pasta-making process than one could ever hope to count. The most difficult part of making pasta is actually deciding to do it - once all the ingredients are in plain sight and you get started, time literally flies. Using a food processor it takes only a few minutes to make the dough and a few more to knead it by hand. Kneading, even when done quickly, cannot and should not be avoided. Pasta dough loves the touch of the hand and working the dough helps to develop gluten, which makes the pasta more elastic.*

Time | 1 hour    Servings | 4

3 eggs
1 tsp extra virgin olive oil
250 g/1⅔ cups flour

Lightly beat the eggs with the oil in a bowl.

Add the flour and eggs to a food processor and blend until the dough comes together. Take out the dough, place it on a floured surface, and knead it for a few minutes until it has a silky smooth surface; it should feel slightly like leather to the touch. Cover with plastic wrap and leave to rest for at least 30 minutes. This step is very important so do not skip it.

After the pasta has rested, divide the dough into 2 parts.

Using a pasta machine or a rolling pin, roll out the pasta fairly thin and then either pass it through the pasta machine to cut it or dust it with flour, roll up loosely and cut it into strips by hand.

Cook the pasta in salted boiling water for 1-2 minutes.

# Busiate

*Pasta loaded with eggs has a wonderful taste all on its own, but in some dishes eggless pasta works just as well, allowing the other ingredients to shine. In Sicily, a great variety of pasta dishes are made with busiate, twisted eggless pasta, which I make at home when I have time to spare and feel like indulging in the flavors of this incredible island.*

*Time* | 1 hour     *Servings* | 4

375g/2 ½ cups durum wheat flour
100-150ml/⅓ – ⅔ cup lukewarm
    water, just enough to make the
    dough sticky

Slowly stir the (lukewarm) water into the flour until the dough has come together, and then knead it for a few minutes. Cover the dough with plastic wrap and let it rest for at least 20 minutes.

After the dough has rested, divide it into 6 parts.

Roll out the pieces, one at a time, to a thickness of about 0.2 inch/0.5 cm and slice them into strips of approximately equal width and about 3 inches/7cm long.

Dust with plenty of flour and roll the strips around a flour-dusted wooden skewer. Once the pasta strip is rolled around the skewer, press it gently down and slide the skewer out, leaving a twisted busiato. Repeat with the remaining dough.

Cook the pasta in plenty of salted boiling water for 1-2 minutes.

# Pasta with swordfish, eggplant and mint

It is far too easy to fall in love with Sicily. Its mesmerizing beauty is matched only by the kindness and hospitality of the people and the most incredible food I have ever had the pleasure of tasting. The extraordinarily colorful history of the island has left its mark on its cuisine and given rise to the most distinctive and unusual flavor combinations. This pasta is a prime example, bringing together local swordfish and eggplant and freshened up with mint. The recipe may sound a little odd, but it is my favorite pasta dish and every time I make it the flavors swing me back to Sicily upon the very first bite..

Time | 50 mins    Servings | 4

1 large swordfish steak, diced into
  1.5 cm/0.6 inch cubes
1 eggplant, diced
120 ml/½ cup sunflower oil
400 g/14 oz busiate or any other
  pasta, preferably eggless
2 tbsp extra virgin olive oil
1 onion, chopped
500 ml/2 cups tomato passata
salt and freshly ground pepper
pinch of sugar
1 garlic clove, lightly crushed
1 tbsp white wine vinegar
a bunch of mint, chopped

Fry the eggplant in sunflower oil until golden brown. Using a slotted spoon, remove the eggplant from the pan and place on a paper towel to absorb any excess oil. You may need to do this in two batches.

Discard the oil, clean the pan, heat 1 tbsp of oil and gently fry the onion for 5-7 minutes until it starts to soften. Stir in the passata and fried eggplant. Season with salt and pepper, add a pinch of sugar and let it simmer for a few minutes.

Cook the pasta in salted water and drain.

In a separate pan, heat a little olive oil and fry the garlic clove on a low heat. When the garlic begins to brown (frying the garlic will infuse the oil), remove the clove from the pan and add the fish.

Toss it around in the frying pan for about a minute and then pour over the vinegar. Shake the pan to coat the fish and then add it to the tomato sauce.

Combine well and let everything simmer for a few minutes, check and adjust the seasoning as required, and finally, stir in the mint and the pasta. Serve immediately.

# Busiate with pesto alla trapanese

On the western shores of Sicily lies Trapani, home to some of the best traditional dishes on the island. Legend has it that merchants from Genoa who passed through the port of Trapani were responsible for bringing the well-known recipe for pesto alla Genovese to the island. The locals took to it immediately and using local produce they made it their own by adding almonds and tomatoes. The results are nothing short of wondrous. The pesto is both fresh and light, and also richly flavorsome, and its uses transcend simple pasta dishes alone as it can also be used as a condiment to dip bread in or for putting the finishing touches to a cooked fish.

Time | 40 mins    Servings | 4

400 g/14 oz busiate, or any other pasta
70 g/2½ oz almonds
4 ripe tomatoes
1 fat garlic clove
a good handful of fresh basil, about 20 leaves
5-7 tablespoons extra virgin olive oil
25 g/¼ cup grated pecorino cheese
Salt and freshly ground pepper

Preheat the oven to 180°C/350°F.
Spread the almonds on a sheet of baking paper and toast in the oven for 5-10 minutes. Let them cool and roughly chop before using in the pesto. To peel the tomatoes, cut a shallow X into the bottom of each one and dip them in boiling water for 30 seconds. Then quickly transfer them to a bowl of ice water to prevent further cooking. Drain, peel, take the seeds out and chop up the flesh.
Add the garlic, almonds, basil and a generous pinch of salt and pepper to a mortar and pound everything until you achieve a paste-like consistency. Gently stir in the olive oil followed by the chopped tomatoes, and finish off with grated pecorino. Taste and adjust the seasoning as required. If using pasta you have bought from the store, cook it according to the instructions on the package; if using fresh pasta, cook it in plenty of salted boiling water for 1-2 minutes. Drain and mix with the pesto. Serve with grated pecorino cheese on top.

# Asparagus, bacon and ricotta pasta

Whenever a recipe calls for ricotta I either make it at home myself or look for one made from sheep's milk at the farmer's market. It is not as widely available in most places as it is in Sicily, where most traditional desserts use this cheese, resulting in the most creamy and delicious sweets and savories. Sheep's milk is naturally richer than cow's milk and the resulting ricotta is both creamier and tastier. When it comes to savories, in Sicily this ricotta is often served with pasta and crisped bacon, but the addition of some lemon and asparagus provides it with even more spring in its step.

Time | 15 mins     Servings | 4

400 g/14 oz spelt pasta
small bunch of asparagus
1 tbsp extra virgin olive oil
150 g/5½ oz diced bacon
250 g/9 oz ricotta
1 lemon, zest only
freshly ground pepper

Boil the pasta in salted water according to the instructions on the package. Before draining, reserve 120 ml/½ cup of the cooking liquid.
Heat a griddle pan and chargrill the oil-brushed asparagus for a few minutes and then slice.
Cook the bacon in a skillet until crisp. Stir in the ricotta and pasta, and season with the lemon zest and pepper. If it looks too dry, tip in a little of the reserved cooking liquid. Taste and adjust the seasoning.
Serve immediately with the grilled asparagus.

Tip 1 | Any pasta will work in this dish but I recommend using spelt pasta, not only because the flavors work really well together but also because it's good to try out new grains from time to time. Spelt pasta is now widely available at most organic supermarkets, but it can also be made at home using the same basic pasta recipe. Just replace wheat flour with spelt four.

Tip 2 | Sheep's milk ricotta is available at most organic stores, or you can source it directly from farmers. My own recipe for ricotta is on page 278

# Shrimps, pistachio and roasted garlic pasta

*This is one of the simplest and quickest yet most delicious pasta dishes and another good reason to always have some roasted garlic sitting in the fridge. Of course, fresh garlic can be used as well, but the sweetness of roasted garlic and the flavor it gives to this dish is without equal. Roasted garlic is good enough to be eaten straight out of the oven with a piece of toasted bread, but it is also almost irreplaceable when making hummus, dips or sauces and whenever a different depth of flavor is required. It is easier to eat pasta when the shrimps have been shelled in advance, but if you don't mind the extra fuss, shrimp shells help flavor the oil and hence the sauce in the most incredible way.*

Time | 15 mins     Servings | 2

250 g/9 oz tagliatelle
3-5 tbsp olive oil
6 roasted garlic cloves, chopped (see page 277)
250 g/9 oz shrimps, (shelled and deveined) or 350 g/12 oz shrimps with shells on
40 g/1½ oz crushed pistachios
250 g/9 oz cherry tomatoes, halved
salt and freshly ground pepper
a few basil leaves, chopped

Boil the pasta according to the instructions in salted water and drain.
Heat 2 tbsp of oil in a pan, add the roasted garlic and shrimps and cook for a few minutes.
Add the pistachios and tomatoes and continue to cook for another 30 seconds, season with salt and pepper, and tip in the cooked pasta. Shake the pan to coat the pasta, add more oil, if needed, and the chopped basil and serve immediately with some extra chopped pistachios on top.

# Squid ink and parsley pasta

*Basil is pasta's most amiable friend, but fresh parsley adds a nice and unexpected kick to pasta dishes and also tends to be cheaper. This dish is as simple as pasta dishes go, but between the tomatoes, fresh parsley and a touch of vinegar there is more flavor to it than meets the eye. As a result, it is my quickest and most delicious dish on the menu in both summer and winter.*

*Time* | 10 mins    *Servings* | 4

250 g/9 oz pasta al Nero di Sepia
  (or any other variety)
12 cherry tomatoes, halved
4 tbsp parsley, chopped
5 tbsp extra virgin olive oil
1-2 tbsp red wine vinegar
salt and freshly ground black pepper
pecorino cheese, shaved (optional)

Boil the pasta is salted water according to the package instructions.
While the pasta is boiling, toss the tomatoes with the parsley, oil and vinegar. Season with salt and pepper. Add the cooked pasta to the tomatoes, give everything a good stir (if it is too dry add more oil), sprinkle with the pecorino shavings and serve immediately.

◄▲►

*Winter version* | Replace fresh tomatoes with sundried ones (quantity according to taste)

# Pappardelle with butternut squash and brown butter cream sauce

Whoever first thought up the idea of heating butter until it turns brown and releases the most alluring nutty aroma deserves a special place in heaven. Roasted pumpkin and amaretti biscuits work impeccably well together and though a little on the sweetish side, when drowned in brown butter (beurre noisette) and sage sauce this is a dish that will enslave all-comers. I cannot emphasize strongly enough how important fresh sage is to this dish; without it all balance and subtlety would be lost.

Time | 1 hour     Servings | 4

1 small butternut squash
extra virgin olive oil
salt and freshly ground pepper
a few sprigs of fresh rosemary
a few leaves of fresh sage
250 g/9 oz fresh or dried pappardelle

**Cream sauce**
60 g/4 tbsp butter
120 ml/½ cup cream
approx. 10 sage leaves, chopped
4-8 crushed amaretti biscuits

Preheat the oven to 180°C/350°F.

Dice the butternut squash into 1.5 cm/0.6 inch cubes. Spread the diced pumpkin on a baking tray, coat with oil, season with salt and pepper, sprinkle with fresh rosemary and sage, and roast for 20-30 minutes.

To make the sauce, melt the butter in a saucepan until the milk solids sink to the bottom and start turning brown. Then add the cream, sage and amaretti (optional), tip in the roasted butternut squash, and cook for another minute. Taste and adjust seasoning as required.

If using freshly made pasta, cook it in salted boiling water for 1-2 minutes, otherwise follow the instructions on the packet. Remove from the water, drain and add directly to the sauce. Serve immediately.

# Guinness and mushroom risotto

*Pasta aside, I think risotto is real lifesaver when you are in need of a quick and delicious meal and don't have much time to spare. The possibilities are also endless. Guinness beer provides a very earthy base and goes perfectly with mushrooms. Be generous with the thyme here - it adds wonderful tone to the dish.*

Time | 30 mins     Servings | 4

45g/3 tbsp butter
250 g/9 oz Portobello or Porcini
  mushrooms, sliced
salt and freshly ground pepper
1 tbsp extra virgin olive oil
1 shallot, diced
200 g/7 oz arborio rice
1 garlic clove, lightly crushed
a few sprigs of fresh thyme
120 ml/½ cup Guinness beer
750 ml – 1 1/3-4 cups warm
  vegetable stock
50 g/½ cup grated parmigiano
  reggiano cheese
1-2 tbsp parsley, chopped

Heat 30 g/2 tbsp of butter in a pan and quickly fry the mushrooms and season with salt and pepper. Set aside.

In the same pan, heat the remaining butter with the oil and cook the shallot for few minutes until softened.

Add the rice, garlic and thyme and cook for another minute, stirring all the time.

Pour in the beer and continue to cook until it has been absorbed, then stir in the stock a spoonful at a time until the rice is cooked. This will take about 20 minutes and you may not need all of the stock.

Once the rice is cooked, remove the garlic clove and thyme, stir in the mushrooms and cheese, taste and adjust the seasoning. Serve with fresh parsley.

# Tagliatelle with black sesame cream sauce

This recipe may be slightly off topic, but I love this pasta dish immensely for its simplicity and surprising flavor. Toasted black sesame seeds give off a lovely nutty aroma and a depth of flavor that when combined with brown butter and cream results in a rich and aromatic dish in the blink of an eye.

**Time** | 15 mins     **Servings** | 4

1 tbsp black sesame seeds, plus extra
   for garnishing
60 g/4 tbsp butter
250 ml/1 cup cream
salt and freshly ground pepper
500 g/18 oz tagliatelle (or any other
   pasta)

Toast the sesame seeds in a dry frying pan for a few minutes on a medium heat, then grind them in a food processor or mortar & pestle.

Melt the butter in a saucepan on a medium high heat until the milk solids have settled on the bottom and it has started to release its nutty aroma. Stir in the cream and the ground sesame seeds, season with salt and pepper and taste.

Cook the pasta in boiling salted water, strain and add to the sauce.

Give everything a good stir, divide between plates, sprinkle with extra sesame seeds and serve immediately.

# Oven-baked gnocchi with porcini and crème fraîche

*The marriage of the humble potato and mushrooms is as classic as it is heavenly, and with a bit of refinement it can become a household staple when autumn knocks on the door bearing all the gifts that wonderful season has to offer. My dish of choice is always fluffy gnocchi, first boiled and then crisped in the oven to perfection and served with a hearty mushroom sauce. Porcini are the most delicious mushrooms and they remind me of when I used to go foraging for them back in Lithuania, which in the fall becomes a kind of national sport for all. Porcini work beautifully in this combination of Italian and French classic dishes, but if they are difficult to come by then Portobello or button mushrooms will make a decent substitute. You can also use gnocchi bought in the store.*

Time | 1 hour    Servings | 4-6

## Gnocchi
1 kg/35 oz potatoes, peeled and diced
2 egg yolks
approx. 200 g/1⅓ cup flour
1-2 tbsp extra virgin olive oil

## Porcini in Crème fraîche
30 g/2 tbsp unsalted butter
1 tsp extra virgin olive oil
1 large onion, finely sliced
350 g/12½ oz large fresh porcini,
   sliced
2 cloves of garlic, finely chopped
120 ml/½ cup white wine
1½ tbsp crème fraiche
2 tbsp sage, chopped
1 tbsp parsley, chopped
Salt and freshly ground pepper

Preheat the oven to 200°C/400°F and line a tray with baking paper.

Place the potatoes in a saucepan, cover with water, add a generous pinch of salt, bring to the boil and simmer for about 20-25 minutes until the potatoes are soft. Drain, mash and pass through a fine sieve. Once the resulting mash has cooled, stir in the egg yolks and the flour, little by little. You have to work the dough quickly and gently, as the more you handle it the tougher it will become. The goal here is to make it using as little flour as possible, which will result in the lightest gnocchi; the more flour you add the heavier and tougher they will be.

Divide the dough into 3-4 parts. On a floured surface, roll each part into a sausage shape about 2cm in diameter and cut the gnocchi out roughly every centimeter or so. To give the gnocchi more texture, press each one against a fork. Bring a large pan of water to the boil and cook the gnocchi until they start to float. Drain and rinse with cold water. Toss with a little olive oil and spread on a prepared tray in a single layer and bake for about 20 minutes, turning them halfway, until they start to get crispy.

In a large non-stick frying pan, melt 1 tablespoon of butter with the oil and fry the onion for about 10-15 minutes, stirring frequently, until caramelized. Set aside. Turn the heat up high, add the remaining butter, and cook the mushrooms for a few minutes, shaking constantly to burn off the moisture and brown the mushrooms a little.

Return the onions to the pan, add the garlic, season with salt and pepper, and cook for 1 more minute. Add the wine, reduce by half, and stir in the crème fraiche. Taste and adjust the seasoning. Finish off the sauce with the sage and parsley and serve with the crispy gnocchi.

# Daily and festive

*I get childishly excited about long meals, about family and friends coming together, where one course follows the next unceasingly, and time flies at the table.*

# Lavender smoked salmon with pickled fennel and whipped labneh

My grandfather was a very handy man. He not only built the house I grew up in, but made lots of additions around it too. One of them was a tiny smoking house where we could smoke our own hams and other kinds of charcuterie. That little addition did not stay with us for long but, some 20 years on, I still remember the smell of the hams smoking - an alluring and intense smoky scent that was dispersed by gusts of wind throughout our backyard, always searching for an opportunity to sneak into the house. Perhaps this is the reason why I love all things smoked and am continuously looking for ways to impart smokiness to the dishes I make. Fortunately, smoking houses aren't a mandatory requirement; all it takes is a heavy pan or wok and lots of herbs or wood chips to do the job. One of my favorites is smoked salmon with very subtle hints of lavender and quick pickled fennel and served with chervil labneh on the side, which brings out the flavor of lavender even more in this dish.

Time | 40 mins    Servings | 4

4 salmon fillets, skin on

**Smoking mix**
4 tbsp uncooked rice
1 tbsp Earl grey tea
4 tbsp lavender
2 tbsp light brown sugar

**Quick pickled fennel**
2 fennel bulbs
8 tbsp white wine vinegar
5 tbsp white sugar
1 tsp salt
zest of 1 orange
1 tsp mustard seeds

**Whipped chervil labneh**
150 g/5½ oz labneh, see recipe
  p 277
2 tsp extra virgin olive oil
pinch of salt
1 tsp sumac
2 tbsp chervil, chopped

Line a cast iron frying pan, wok or heavy bottomed casserole with 4 large sheets of aluminum foil overlapping the sides. Add the smoking mix, place a rack/grid in the pan and turn the heat up to high. When you see smoke starting to rise, place the salmon fillets on the rack, cover everything tightly with a lid, and wrap the sides with the foil (to prevent the smoke from escaping). Continue to smoke for about 15 minutes, then remove from the heat and leave covered for another 15 minutes.

While the salmon is smoking, slice the fennel as thinly as possible (I recommend using a mandolin). Bring the rest of the ingredients to the boil until the sugar and salt have dissolved and then tip in the fennel and set aside to cool; drain after 20 minutes.

Whip together the labneh, oil, salt and sumac and stir in the chervil.

Serve the smoked salmon with whipped labneh and pickled fennel on the side.

# Grand aioli

A good aioli is often hard to come by. Too many restaurants in the South of France tone down the garlic in an attempt to please the masses, which goes against the very grain of what aioli is all about. My father-in-law holds the monopoly on aioli-making in our family, and rightly so, as his recipe is as good as they come and lends a whole new meaning to the word "garlicky". Aioli served together with seafood, vegetables and eggs is known as Grand Aioli, a rather quintessential Provencal platter that combines the very best flavors of the region. Served with a chilled rosé and a fresh baguette, it is an excellent summer dish for enjoying with family and friends, and it may even help you make new ones. As a sauce, aioli can be as strong or as light in terms of its garlic flavor as individual preferences go. For a medium strength, one fat garlic clove per person will suffice, and it will be fantastic not only with this platter but also with grilled fish, shellfish and even cold meats, or just as something for dipping your bread in.

Time | 1 hour    Servings | 4

## Aioli

4 fat garlic cloves, roughly chopped
pinch of coarse salt
small handful of stale bread, soaked
    in milk
1 egg yolk
160 ml/⅔ cup extra virgin olive oil
120 ml/½ cup sunflower oil
1-2 tsp red wine vinegar

## Platter

a few potatoes
4 eggs
½ head of cauliflower, cut into florets
a few handfuls of green beans
2-3 carrots, halved and quartered
4 small cod fillets
16-24 pre-cooked whelks

To make the aioli, use a pestle and mortar to pound the garlic with the salt until it has achieved a paste-like consistency. Squeeze any extra milk out of the bread and pound it together with the garlic and egg yolk to a smooth paste. Start adding the oils, only a few drops at a time, and stir continuously to prevent the aioli from splitting. After about 80 ml of the oil has been incorporated, the rest can be added in larger amounts. Taste, and if the aioli is too strong add more oil. Finish off by adding 1-2 teaspoons of red wine vinegar.

To prepare the platter, boil the potatoes and eggs to your liking. Boil or steam the cauliflower, beans and carrots until just tender. This will take between 3-6 minutes if steaming or up to 10 minutes if boiling, so keep an eye on the clock. The beans will cook the quickest, while the cauliflower will take the longest. If steaming, it is best to do so over fish stock with a few bay leaves thrown in. If boiling, be sure to add salt to the water.

Steam the cod for 5-7 minutes, depending on how large the pieces are. Serve the platter with freshly made aioli, a fresh baguette or two and a bottle of chilled rosé.

# Braised octopus

*Braised octopus never fails to remind me of Sardinia; crisp early September evenings in the mountains when the heat of the day has subsided and a mountain chill slowly creeps in; when a steaming bowl of rich braised octopus is the perfect accompaniment to sitting outside and watching the colors change on the horizon.*

*Time* | 2½ hour     *Servings* | 4

1 kg/35 oz octopus, legs only
2 tbsp extra virgin olive oil
1 onion, finely chopped
12 garlic cloves, sliced
pinch of dried pepperoncini
200 ml/¾ cups red wine
800 g/28 oz ripe tomatoes, roughly
   chopped
1 tsp sugar
zest of 1 orange
salt and freshly ground pepper
a large handful of parsley

Heat the oil in a casserole and fry the onion until soft, then add the garlic and pepperoncino and stir for a minute or two more. Add the wine, tomatoes, sugar and zest. Leave to simmer gently. Carefully slice the octopus into chunks. Season with salt and pepper and leave to simmer for about 1½-2 hours on a very gentle heat, making sure that the octopus is covered with liquid at all times. Add a little water if needed. Check the octopus by piercing it with a fork at the thickest part; the fork should come out easily and the octopus should feel soft to the touch. Taste the sauce and adjust the seasoning. Sprinkle with parsley and serve with bread.

# Cod 'en papillote'

*En Papillote means cooking something wrapped in baking paper, sadly a much-underused technique. All it takes is to wrap whatever you want to cook - in this case a humble cod - tightly in baking paper and let the oven to do the rest. I love cod cooked in a simple sweet and sour onion and pepper sauce, but if you're short on time you can roast it with cherry tomatoes, some pesto or just plenty of herbs and extra virgin olive oil. This is a perfect technique when cooking fish for a dinner party. But when baking six or more parcels do remember that the fish might take a little longer to cook.*

Time | 40 mins     Servings | 4

4 cod fillets

extra virgin olive oil

3 large onions, halved and sliced

salt and freshly ground black pepper

1½ tbsp white caster sugar

3-5 tbsp white wine vinegar

4 roasted bell peppers, see recipe on p. 46

4 sprigs of fresh thyme

Preheat the oven to 190°C/375°F.

Heat 3 tbsp of oil in a pan and fry the onions on a low-medium heat, stirring occasionally, until they start to caramelize. This will take about 15-20 minutes. Season with salt and pepper and then add the sugar, 3 tbsp of vinegar and the sliced bell peppers. Cook for a few minutes and taste to check the balance of sweet and sour. You may need to add more vinegar if it's too sweet or more sugar if it's too sour.

Prepare 4 pieces of baking paper and divide the pepper onion sauce between them. Top each one with a fillet of cod, black pepper, salt and a sprig of thyme. Starting from one corner, carefully fold over the edges to seal the parcel. Repeat with the rest of the fish. Place all of the parcels on a tray lined with baking paper and bake for 10 minutes. Once out of the oven let them rest for a few minutes before serving.

# Fish couscous

*Every September in the northwestern part of Sicily, a festival takes over the streets of San Vito Lo Capo (you could even call it an ode to couscous). A legacy of Moorish rule, couscous has carved out a prominent place for itself in Sicilian cuisine, and every year chefs from all over Sicily and also from neighboring countries gather to showcase the possibilities of this humble dish; one that is rich in history and adept at binding cultures together.*

*Time* | 1 hour 30 mins     *Servings* | 4

2 kg/4 lb and 2 oz fish

2 squids, cleaned and sliced into rings (optional)

300 g/10½ oz shrimps, shells on

210 g/7½ oz/1 cup plus 2 tbsp couscous

5 medium-sized tomatoes

2 medium-sized onions

3 tbsp olive oil

80 g/3 oz almonds

10 garlic cloves

3 tbsp parsley, chopped

pinch of pepperoncino

3 tbsp tomato paste

2 bay leaves

salt and freshly ground pepper

Blend the tomatoes and set aside.

Mince the onions in a food processor.

In a large casserole, heat the oil and cook the onion on a low-to-medium heat for about 5 minutes.

Blend the almonds, garlic and parsley in the food processor until they have achieved an almost paste-like consistency and add to the onions along with a pinch of pepperoncino. Cook it for about a minute, stir in the tomato paste and tomatoes, and top up with 2 liters of water. Add the bay leaves, season with salt and pepper and leave to simmer.

In the meantime, fillet the fish and add the heads and bones to the casserole. Set the fillets aside. Cook the stock for about 50 minutes on a medium-high heat. The idea is to get the fish to start disintegrating and add some serious flavor to the stock.

Pass the stock through a rough sieve and discard the fish bones. Measure out 450 ml/1⅔ cups of stock and pour this over the couscous, cover, and set aside.

Add the squid rings to the rest of the stock and allow to simmer for 10 minutes, then add the shrimps before adding the fish fillets 5 minutes later. Continue to cook for 3-5 more minutes, then scoop all the seafood out, transfer to a plate, and keep warm.

Turn the heat up and reduce the sauce for a few minutes before serving on the side with the couscous and fish.

# Oven-baked sea bream

*I think sea bream always calls for bold companions like orange, ginger and chili to balance its milky and delicate nature. I use reduced fresh orange juice here, as it carries so much more flavor than you get from squeezing an orange straight onto the fish. It is definitely worth waiting the few minutes extra it takes to reduce the juice properly. Prepared this way, all that sea bream needs once out of the oven is some fresh cilantro and a couple of hungry fish lovers.*

Time | 35 mins    Servings | 2

2 whole sea breams, cleaned
250 ml/1 cup fresh orange juice,
   from about 4 oranges
zest of 1 orange
1½ tbsp soy sauce
1 chili, finely chopped
1 tbsp of ginger, chopped
2 garlic cloves, chopped
1 tbsp extra virgin olive oil
fresh cilantro to serve

Set the oven grill to high.

In a saucepan, bring the orange juice and zest to the boil and reduce until only about 4 tbsp remain. Stir in the soy sauce, garlic, ginger and chili.

On a baking tray, place the fish on separate oiled aluminum sheets. Pour over the orange sauce, fold up the sides of the foil a little so that the sauce won't spill out, but without covering the fish, and grill for about 10-15 minutes.

Serve immediately with fresh cilantro on top.

# Moules frites with shrimp bisque

In the old port of Marseille, nestled between the florid and faded facades and right on the steps of the famous fish market, countless little restaurants go about their daily business in a highly animated fashion. Seafood is the star on each menu here - to varying degrees of excellence - but one restaurant has mastered the art of serving the perfect moules frites, a dish that brings me back to Marseille again and again looking for more. After all, when there is lobster bisque involved, what is there not to love? In honor of this delicacy, I often make my own version at home. Shrimps make a more humble but still delicious bisque and they are more readily available, but it almost goes without saying that lobster would work just marvelously here too, of course.

Time | 45 mins     Servings | 2

1 kg/28 oz fresh mussels
2 tbsp parsley, chopped

**Shrimp bisque**
300 g/10½ oz shrimps, shells on
2 tbsp extra virgin olive oil
1 onion, diced
3 garlic cloves, chopped
pinch of chili flakes
1 tbsp tomato paste
120 ml/½ cup white wine
360 ml/1½ cups chicken stock
2 tbsp crème fraiche

**Frites**
3 medium-sized potatoes, sliced
oil for frying
salt

Place the mussels into a large bowl of cold water. Discard any that remain open when tapped, drain, and pull away any 'beards'; set aside. As with any type of fish, a smell of 'fishiness' is a sign that they are no longer fresh, so avoid those at all costs.

For the bisque, remove the shells and devein the shrimps. In a large frying pan, heat the oil and fry the shells and the onions very gently for a few minutes. Add the garlic and chili flakes and cook for one minute more.

Finally, stir in the tomato paste, coating everything, and pour in the white wine. Let it cook for a minute or so, then stir in the stock and crème fraiche. Let it simmer for 15-20 minutes. Do not add any salt; the mussels themselves will be salty enough. Pass the shrimp bisque through a fine sieve and set aside.

Heat a deep pan until smoking hot and add the cleaned mussels. Toss them around, cover, and cook on a high heat for about 4 minutes. Drain all the liquid from the mussels, add the shrimp bisque to the saucepan, coating the cooked mussels thoroughly, and allow everything to come up to temperature.

Fry the potatoes and place on a paper towel to soak up any excess oil; sprinkle with a little salt.

Before serving, discard any mussels that have not opened, sprinkle with fresh parsley and serve.

# Cod in creamy vanilla sauce

*Pairing fish with vanilla is not everybody's cup of tea. Some say it should never get anywhere near the kitchen and others say it's a remarkable combination that should be celebrated. I belong to the latter camp and believe that, when done well, fish and vanilla can conjure up a little taste of heaven.*

Time | 20 mins    Servings | 4

4 fillets of cod (about 180 g each)
knob of butter
2 shallots, diced
1 vanilla pod
3 tbsp white wine
80 ml/⅓ cup vegetable stock
250 ml/1 cup almond milk
1 tsp corn starch
salt and freshly ground pepper
1 cauliflower head
handful of almonds, toasted and
  chopped
fresh cilantro

In a large frying pan, melt the butter and fry the shallots for 2-3 minutes. Split the vanilla pod, scrape out the seeds and add to the shallots, along with the pod. Stir in the white wine and leave to simmer for 1-2 minutes. Finally, pour in the stock and the milk and bring to a gentle simmer, stirring frequently. Taste and adjust the seasoning.

Once this is simmering nicely, gently slide in the fish fillets and let them cook for about 3 minutes. When they flake easily they are ready. Transfer the fish onto a plate and keep warm.

Stir the corn starch into the sauce, bring the heat up and stir continuously until the sauce has thickened a little.

To prepare the cauliflower, cut it into uniform pieces and boil or steam until tender. Depending on the size of florets this can take between 5-10 minutes.

Serve the fish with the cauliflower, almond flakes and some chopped cilantro on top.

# Stuffed mackerel

*The best way to enjoy baked mackerel is to add a bit of crunchy stuffing and a sweet and sour topping. Fatty, filling and blessed with nature's finest flavors, mackerel doesn't need much help to be delicious, and I love just how quickly it can be prepared.*

**Time** | 40 mins  **Servings** | 2

*2 mackerels, cleaned*
*2-3 tbsp garlic oil*
*2 tbsp extra virgin olive oil*
*zest and juice of 1 lemon*
*4 tbsp chopped parsley*
*4 garlic cloves, chopped*
*30 g/1 oz breadcrumbs*
*30 g/1 oz pine nuts*
*salt and freshly ground pepper*
*150 g/5½ oz cherry tomatoes, halved*

**Pickled cucumber**
*1 large cucumber*
*2 tbsp white wine vinegar*
*1½ tbsp sugar*

Preheat the oven to 200°C/400°F.

Mix together the oil, lemon juice, 2 tablespoons of the parsley and the garlic.

Wash the mackerels thoroughly and pat dry, score the skin a few times on both sides, rub with the garlic oil all over and place on a baking tray.

Toss together the breadcrumbs, pine nuts, remaining parsley and lemon zest. Season liberally with salt and pepper and use to stuff the mackerels. Some of the stuffing will fall out, but that's okay. Scatter the tomato halves around the fish and drizzle with a little more olive oil before finishing with a little salt and pepper. Bake for 20-25 minutes.

Slice the cucumber as thinly as possible (a mandolin is handy here). Heat the vinegar and sugar until the sugar has dissolved and then pour over the sliced cucumber. Drain just before serving.

Serve the baked mackerel with the pickled cucumber and fresh bread or boiled potatoes.

# Grilled sea bass with almonds and brown butter

*I love the smell of nutty brown butter, which goes fabulously with just about anything and is magical when used with fish. This is a variation of the classic sole meunière - in spirit at least. To stick to the more classical route, just dust the fish in flour and pan-fry it. However, grilling it in the oven is a much simpler way to cook a whole fish and produce a fabulous fuss-free dinner in minutes.*

Time | 20 mins    Servings | 2

2 sea bass, whole, cleaned
2 tbsp extra virgin olive oil
salt and freshly ground pepper
a few sprigs of fresh thyme

**Brown butter sauce**
60 g/4 tbsp butter
70 g/2½ oz sliced almonds
salt
1 tbsp lemon juice
2 tbsp chopped parsley

Turn the oven grill to high. Rinse the sea bass and pat dry. Line a baking tray with foil, rub the sea bass with oil and score the skin in a few spots on top; sprinkle with salt and pepper. Season the cavity of the fish, place a few sprigs of thyme inside and scatter a few more on top.
Grill for about 10 minutes.
To make the sauce, melt the butter in a saucepan on a medium-to-high heat until it begins to release its nutty aroma. Add the almonds and a little salt and cook for about one minute more. Remove from the heat, stir in the lemon juice and parsley, and pour over the grilled fish and serve.

◄▲►

*Variation* | Grilled sea bass can be served with just about any sauce, such as ravigote (see page 186) *for a lighter meal.*

◄▲►

*Tip* | The same dish can be made with trout.

# Mediterranean fish stew

*Whenever I visit Marseille I cannot wait to dig into its celebrated bouillabaisse. Every spoonful tastes like a gathering of the best flavors of the Mediterranean. It is an experience in itself, not just a source of nourishment, and no praise can be considered high enough. Back home, when haunted by memories of Marseille's bouillabaisse, I make this fish stew in an attempt to satisfy my yearnings. It is not, admittedly, the real thing described above, which would take up more much more time and demand a heavier market basket, but it has layer upon layer of flavors and never fails to remind me of the Mediterranean coast.*

**Time** | 1 hour 15 mins          **Servings** | 4-6

1.3 kg/3 lb of various fish (cod, sole, halibut, sea bass), cut into chunks
200 g/7 oz shrimps, shells on
2 bell peppers
olive oil
fresh basil leaves

**Shellfish sauce**
3 tbsp extra virgin olive oil
1 shallot, chopped
3 garlic cloves, chopped
1 tbsp tomato paste
120 ml/½ cup white wine
pinch of sugar
pinch of chili flakes

**Stock**
1 medium-sized onion, diced
2 small carrots, diced
2 celery sticks, diced
1 fennel bulb, diced
2 bay leaves
a pinch of saffron
2 fresh tomatoes, peeled and quartered
salt and freshly ground pepper

Half and core the bell peppers, rub with olive oil and place under a hot grill until they start to blacken. Place them in a bowl and cover with plastic wrap for 5 minutes. This will help to loosen the skin. Peel, slice and set aside.

Shell and devein the shrimps. Add 3 tbsp of oil to a frying pan, set to a medium-high heat and briefly fry the shrimp. Then add the shallot and garlic and continue to fry for another 3 minutes.

Set aside 2 tablespoons of oil from the pan, stir in the tomato paste and coat everything, pour in the wine and let it cook for about a minute. Add a good pinch of sugar and the chili flakes and top up with 250 ml/1 cup water. Leave to simmer for 15-20 minutes. Keep an eye on it as you may need to add some extra water if it becomes too dry. Then pass through a fine sieve.

In a large casserole, heat 2 tablespoons of the shrimp-flavored oil and gently sauté the onion for a few minutes. Add the carrots and celery and continue to cook for a few more minutes. Add the fennel, pour in 1 liter of water, and then add the bay leaves, a pinch of saffron and the tomatoes and simmer for about 20 minutes. Stir in the shellfish sauce, taste and adjust the seasoning. Add the fish chunks, shrimps and roasted bell peppers, cover, and leave to simmer for about 5 minutes. Sprinkle the fish stew with fresh basil leaves and serve with lots of bread.

# Clams in almond and parsley sauce

*I love the simplicity of this dish and how incredibly quickly it comes together, with smashingly delicious results.*

Time | 15 mins     Servings | 4

1 kg/35 oz clams, cleaned

1 shallot, roughly chopped

4 garlic cloves, chopped

60 g/4 tbsp almonds, toasted and
  chopped

a generous handful of parsley,
  chopped

4 tbsp extra virgin olive oil

pinch of saffron

salt and freshly ground pepper

1-2 tbsp lemon juice

400 g/14 oz boiled new potatoes or
  pasta to serve

Blend together the shallot, garlic, almonds, parsley and oil until you have a consistent green sauce.

Heat a deep pan until very hot, add the sauce and the saffron and fry for one minute, stirring continuously. Tip in the cleaned clams, shake to coat in the sauce and leave to cook for about 4-6 minutes until all the clams have opened up.

Scoop the clams out of the pan and onto prepared plates, taste the sauce and adjust the seasoning, and finish off with a drop or two of lemon juice. Pour the sauce over the clams and serve immediately with potatoes or pasta.

# Beer-braised chicken

*I am not sure when I first substituted dark ale for wine in coq au vin - it might have been an experiment of some sort - but it became an instant favorite of mine. The result is both delightful and heartwarming, and beer adds a nice earthy note to this wonderful chicken stew.*

Time | 1 hour    Servings | 2

2 chicken legs, preferably free range,
   at room temperature
salt and freshly ground pepper
1 tbsp extra virgin olive oil
100 g/3½ oz diced bacon
2 large onions, peeled, halved and
   thinly sliced
1 tsp brown sugar
2 tbsp Dijon mustard
300 ml/1¼ cup dark brown ale
120 ml/½ cup beef stock
a few sprigs of thyme
a few sprigs of rosemary
1 bay leaf

**Crispy potatoes**
500 g/18 oz potatoes, peeled and cut
   in half (all same size)
2-3 tbsp olive oil
Salt and freshly ground pepper
a few sprigs of fresh rosemary,
   chopped

Start by preparing the potatoes. Preheat the oven to 220°C/430°F and place the tray you will be using for the potatoes in the oven to warm up. Cover the potatoes with cold water and bring to the boil with a pinch of salt. Drain immediately and rinse the potatoes in cold water. Take the hot tray out of the oven, pour in the olive oil, sprinkle in some salt and pepper, add the rosemary and shake the tray to mix everything together. Tip in the potatoes carefully, coating them in the oil, and arrange cut-side down.

Bake in the oven for about 35 minutes. The exact baking time depends on your oven but check them anyway about 20 minutes into baking. If the bottoms are browning too much, turn them over for the remainder of the baking time.

Season the chicken legs with salt and pepper. Heat the oil in a casserole and fry the chicken legs on both sides until golden brown (about 2-3 minutes each side). Set aside. In the same casserole, fry the bacon for 2-3 minutes, add the onions and, stirring frequently, fry for another 5-8 minutes on a high heat until they start to caramelize. Then stir in the brown sugar and mustard. Pour in the beer and let it bubble for a minute, followed by the stock. Add the thyme, rosemary, bay leaf and chicken legs. Cover and simmer for 25-30 minutes until the chicken is almost falling off the bone.

You'll probably still have too much sauce, so take out the chicken legs and reduce the sauce on a high heat by about half. This also helps to concentrate the flavor. Taste, and adjust the seasoning if required. Return the chicken to the pan and serve with the crispy rosemary potatoes.

# Chicken with romesco sauce

*I could probably eat romesco sauce all by itself, given it has the consistency of a very thick soup and is irreplaceable in summer. Sometimes it is best served with nothing more complicated than freshly boiled green beans and a little feta cheese on top. For a more filling meal I serve it with pan-seared chicken breast, which I like to marinate for 24 hours in a smoky tea marinade (see page 179) for a very moist and tender chicken breast. Pasta and potatoes work perfectly as sides here, but eggplant fries (see page 43) are to die for..*

Time | 1 hour   Servings | 4

4 boneless, skinless chicken breasts
2 tbsp extra virgin olive oil
30 g/2 tbsp butter
2 garlic cloves, halved
a few sprigs of thyme
salt and freshly ground black pepper

**Romesco sauce**
3 bell peppers, halved
2-4 tbsp extra virgin olive oil
2 tomatoes, halved
4 medium garlic cloves
40 g/1½ oz almonds, chopped and
    roasted
A handful of basil leaves
salt and freshly ground black pepper

For the romesco sauce, halve and core the bell peppers and place them cut-side down on a baking tray lined with aluminum foil; rub with a little olive oil. Add the halved tomatoes (cut-side up) and garlic (not peeled) and cook everything under a hot grill until the pepper skins start to blacken. Note: garlic may take less time to cook; it is done when soft inside to the touch.

Transfer the bell peppers to a bowl and cover them with plastic wrap. This will help to loosen their skins and make peeling easier. Squeeze the garlic out of their skins. Peel the tomatoes and keep them warm. After 3-5 minutes, peel the peppers and add to a blender along with the tomatoes, roughly chopped almonds, fresh basil, peeled garlic and 2 tablespoons of olive oil; season with salt and pepper and blend for 5-10 seconds. I like the sauce to be quite chunky, but you can make it to your own liking. Taste and adjust the seasoning.

Heat the oven to 180°C/350°F.

To cook the chicken, heat a frying pan until smoking hot. Add the oil, butter, garlic and thyme to the pan. Season the chicken breasts generously with salt and pepper and sear each side until golden brown. Place the pan in the oven and continue to cook for another 10-15 minutes. Ovens do vary with regard to cooking times, so keep a sharp eye on the chicken breasts. Serve immediately with romesco sauce.

# Chicken drumsticks with roasted garlic cauliflower mash

*This is a swift dish that requires very little effort, but the results are nonetheless delicious. Using cauliflower instead of regular potato mash makes for a lighter and perhaps healthier alternative, but don't be too stingy with the roasted garlic. Chicken drumsticks can easily be replaced with chicken legs; just remember to increase the cooking time by a few minutes.*

Time | 1 hour    Servings | 4

8-12 chicken drumsticks (2-3 per
  person, depending on size)
1 lemon, zest and juice
4 tbsp extra virgin olive oil
salt and freshly ground pepper
a bunch of thyme
4 garlic cloves

### Cauliflower mash
1 large head of cauliflower
500-750 ml/2-3 cups chicken stock
30 g/2 tbsp cold butter

Preheat the oven to 200°C/400°F.

Mix together the lemon juice, zest and oil and toss with the chicken drumsticks. Season with salt and pepper and roughly chopped thyme. Leave to marinate for at least 15 minutes.

Arrange the drumsticks on a baking tray, pour over the remaining marinade, scatter the garlic cloves (skins on) on top and roast for 40-45 minutes.

Cut the cauliflower into equal-sized florets and cook them in the chicken stock for 5-7 minutes until tender; then drain, reserving the chicken stock.

Blend the cauliflower in a food processor with the peeled roasted garlic cloves and about 80 ml/⅓ cup of the chicken stock. Add more stock if needed and then stir in the cold butter. Taste and adjust the seasoning. Serve the roasted chicken drumsticks with the cauliflower mash and drizzle with the roasting juices.

# Chicken with port wine and mushroom Sauce

*I keep a bottle of Port wine in the pantry so I can cook this dish anytime I feel like it. With the help of a sweet and flavorsome Port wine, this delicious dish, worthy of dinner parties, can be ready within minutes, but it is also handy for a weeknight meal.*

**Time** | 25 mins    **Servings** | 2

*2 skinless, boneless chicken breasts*
*30 g/2 tbsp butter*
*salt and freshly ground pepper*
*200 g/7 oz button mushrooms, sliced*
*160 ml/⅔ cup Port wine*
*80 ml/⅓ cup cream*
*Boiled rice, to serve*
*fresh parsley*

Melt the butter in a frying pan, season the chicken and cook it on both sides for 3-5 minutes until nicely brown. Remove the chicken from the pan and set aside.

In the same pan, brown the mushrooms; you may need to do this in two batches, depending on the size of your pan, as if you add too many mushrooms at a they will only cook in their own juices instead of browning. Add more butter if needed.

When the mushrooms have browned, add the Port wine and let it bubble for a couple of minutes.

Stir in the cream, return the chicken to the pan, and cook for another minutes or just long enough to allow the sauce to thicken. Taste and adjust the seasoning.

Serve the chicken with boiled rice and a sprinkling of parsley.

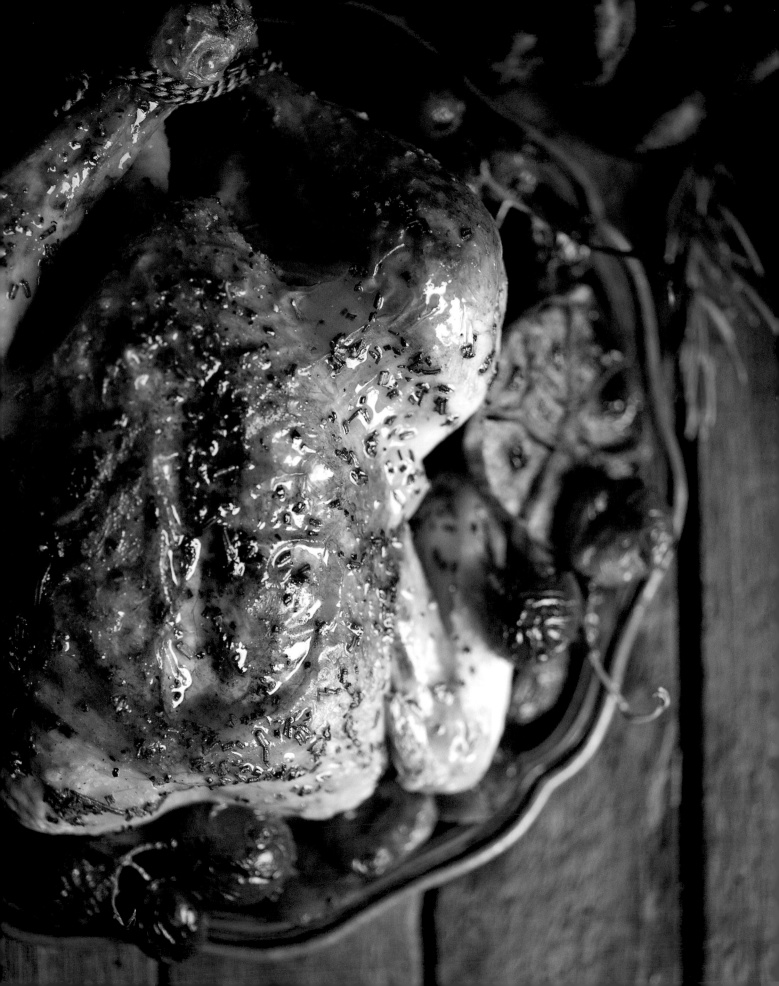

# Tea-roasted chicken with grapes

This, without a doubt, is one the best roast chicken dishes out there, or at least for me it is. My secret ingredient is smoky black tea from China - Lapsang Souchong - which is fortunately widely available and stocked by most tea shops. The chicken is brined overnight in the aromatic liquid, which results not only in the most moist and succulent chicken but also imparts a delicate smoky flavor that permeates every bite. The rosemary, grapes and butter sauce marries perfectly with the delicate chicken, creating a symphony of flavors that linger in the mouth long after the meal is finished.

Time | 2 hours      Servings | 4

1.5 kg/3 lb and 5 oz chicken
5 tbsp lapsang souchong tea
4 tbsp salt
2 tbsp brown sugar
1 cinnamon stick
1 star anise
1 tsp black peppercorns
1 lemon, sliced
a bunch of fresh rosemary
60 g/4 tbsp butter, softened
200 g/7 oz grapes
4 garlic cloves, halved
1 tbsp extra virgin olive oil
½ kg/18 oz potatoes

The day before cooking, add the tea to 1.5 liters/6 cups of boiling water, cover, and let it steep for 6 minutes. Discard the tea leaves and then add the salt, sugar, cinnamon stick, star anise and peppercorns. Let it simmer for 5 minutes, then remove from the heat and leave to cool to room temperature. Drain, and reserve the liquid.

Put the chicken in a double ziplock bag, pour in the marinade (making sure it covers all of chicken) and leave to marinate in the fridge for 24 hours.

On the day of cooking, preheat the oven to 180°C/350°F. Remove the chicken from the marinade and pat it dry. Stuff it with the lemon and rosemary, then rub with 30 g of the butter.

Halve the grapes, remove the seeds and scatter around the chicken along with the garlic, then brush the grapes with a little more butter. Place in the oven for 75-90 minutes.

Once out of the oven, flip the chicken over, cover with foil and a tea towel and allow to rest for at least 15 minutes; 30 is even better. Turn the oven up to 220°C/430°F.

Dice the potatoes, place in a saucepan with cold water and bring to the boil. Then drain and rinse with cold water and leave to dry for a few minutes. Toss the potatoes with the oil and the remaining butter, season with salt and pepper and bake for 30 minutes until crispy and golden brown (do this while the chicken is resting).

Serve the roasted chicken with the grapes, potatoes and the juices from the meat.

# Bacon-wrapped chicken terrine with pistachios

*This is a terrific terrine. Christmas, Easter or any other festive occasion in our home wouldn't be the same without it. Wrapped in bacon that crisps up during cooking, the chicken remains succulent inside, and when served with red wine onion jam (see page 65) or horseradish lime cream (see page 54), or even both, it's a pure delight.*

**Time** | 1 hour 25 mins       **Servings** | 6-8

700 g/25 oz minced chicken
1 tbsp butter
1 tsp extra virgin olive oil
1 onion, finely diced
1 medium-sized carrot, grated
1 stick of celery, finely chopped
1 small parsnip, grated
3 cloves of garlic, chopped
2 tbsp chopped fresh rosemary
1 tbsp mayonnaise
1 tbsp semolina or breadcrumbs
1 tbsp Dijon mustard
salt and freshly ground pepper
1 egg
1 pack of streaky bacon
120 g/4 oz toasted pistachios, chopped

Preheat the oven to 190°C/375°F.

Heat the oil and butter in a frying pan and sauté the onions, carrots, celery, parsnip and garlic for a few minutes; season with salt and pepper. Add the rosemary at the very end.

Allow to cool a little before adding to the mince.

Thoroughly mix all of the ingredients for the terrine, except for the bacon and pistachios, and season with salt and pepper.

Line a 21.5 x 11 cm/8½ x 4 inch terrine case (750 ml/3 cups) with baking paper and arrange the slices of bacon so that they are overlapping on each side.

Add ⅔ of the terrine mixture to the case, sprinkle with the pistachios and then add the remaining mince.

Fold the bacon over on top and cover with aluminum foil.

Bake for 45 minutes, then remove the foil and bake for another 10 minutes until the bacon crisps up.

Serve the terrine warm or cold.

# Turkey escallops with chestnuts and apples

*Fall is a happy season for chestnuts lovers, as these little gems work marvelously in both sweet and savory dishes, and in the company of apples and cider you can literally eat the season off your plate.*
*This is probably one of the quickest turkey dishes around and it can be prepared in less than 20 minutes. The same sauce can also be used with chicken. You can buy the chestnuts already cooked if you wish, but it is very easy to prepare them at home.*

*Time* | 20 mins     *Servings* | 2

300 g/10½ oz turkey breast
salt and freshly ground black pepper
45 g/3 tbsp butter
1 onion, halved and thinly sliced
1 Jonagold apple, sliced into 8-10
  wedges
200 g/7 oz chestnuts, roasted
250 ml/1 cup dry apple cider
80 ml/⅓ cup cream
7 sage leaves, chopped

Slice the turkey breast into four pieces, place them between sheets of plastic wrap and use a rolling pin to flatten them out a little; season with salt and pepper.

Heat half of the butter in a frying pan and fry the turkey slices on a medium-high heat for about 30 seconds on each side. Set aside.

Add a little more butter to the pan and, stirring all the time, fry the onions until they have caramelized. Remove from the pan and set aside. Heat the remaining butter in the pan and quickly fry the apples on a high heat. Then return the caramelized onions to the pan, add the chestnuts, pour in the cider and let it all reduce until about ⅓ of the liquid remains. Stir in the cream and sage, taste, and adjust the seasoning if required. Return the turkey slices to the pan to coat and reheat them. At this point do not cook the turkey for more than 2-3 minutes or it will overcook and turn dry.

Serve as is or with bread.

◀▶

*Tip* | Chestnuts can be roasted by making a shallow X in their skins and roasting them for about 15-20 minutes in an oven preheated to 200°C/400°

# Magret de canard with plum sauce and parsnip purée

*The memories of my first taste of magret de canard go hand in hand with my first ever trip to France. It was the end of summer and I found myself sitting with the friends and family of my husband-to-be around the table at a lovely feast under the Provence sun; all chat and laughter and everything a proper long lunch should entail. It wasn't until we were well into the meal, and long after all the introductions and 'enchantés' had passed and the wine had quickened our tongues, that I realized two things. First, that my French was nowhere near as good as I had imagined it to be, and second, that I will never ever look at magret de canard in the same way again.*

**Time** | 45 mins    **Servings** | 4

4 duck breasts, skin on
1 or two sprigs of thyme
1 garlic clove, lightly crushed
salt and freshly ground pepper

### Parsnip purée
4 very large parsnips or 8-12 small
  ones
500 ml/2 cups chicken stock
15-60 g/3-4 tbsp butter

### Port wine sauce
1 tbsp extra virgin olive oil
1 shallot, finely chopped
1 garlic clove, lightly crushed
1 sprig of thyme
2-4 red plums, cut into wedges
160 ml/⅔ cups Port wine
250 ml/1 cup red wine
250 ml/1 cup beef stock
Salt and freshly ground pepper
15-30 g/1-2 tbsp butter

Peel the parsnips, slice them into large chunks, and cook them in the chicken stock until tender. Drain, reserving the stock, and blend with 45g/3 tbsp butter and a little stock until very creamy and smooth. Add more stock or butter if needed and set aside.

For the sauce, heat the oil in a saucepan and fry the shallots for a few minutes. Then add 1 garlic clove, some of the thyme and the plums, season with salt and pepper and continue to cook for another minute.

Add the port wine, red wine and stock and simmer until reduced by about two thirds (will take 15-25 minutes).

Remove the garlic and thyme and just before serving whisk the butter into the hot sauce.

Once the sauce is cooking, start on the duck. Lightly score the skin and season both sides with salt and pepper.

Lay the duck breast skin-side down in a cold pan and place on a medium heat. When the fat starts to separate add the remaining garlic and thyme to the pan, turn the heat down and continue to cook for about 15 minutes until the skin is nice and crispy.

Flip the duck onto the flesh side and continue to cook for another 3-5 minutes, depending on the size of the breast and how pink you like your duck. 2-3 minutes is enough for medium rare and 5 for well done.

Remove from the pan and leave to rest in a warm spot for a few minutes, skin-side up.

Serve the duck with the parsnip puree and your rich Port wine sauce.

# Beef with sauce ravigote

When spring and summer are on their way I slowly abandon cream and transfer my affections to olive oil. Creamy pastas are abandoned and even meat calls for lighter company. Ravigote is one of those French classics of which there are countless variations. It literally means "freshened up", which is exactly what it does to any dish it touches. It's fantastic with fish and poultry, but my favorite partner is a juicy steak and roasted vegetables, making a dish that is both fresh and filling. I like to heat my sauce just a little, but it can also be served cold with hot meat and vegetables.

Time | 1 hour     Servings | 2

2 beef steaks
2 large potatoes, peeled and cut into wedges
4 tbsp extra virgin olive oil
salt and freshly ground pepper
1 turnip, peeled and cut into large chunks
2 medium-sized carrots, peeled and cut into chunks
2-4 small beets
1 head of broccoli, cut into florets
a little sunflower oil for rubbing on the steak
10 g/½ tbsp of butter

**Sauce Ravigote**
6 tbsp extra virgin olive oil
1 small shallot, finely diced
4 anchovy fillets, minced
1 tbsp of capers
zest of 1 lemon
2 tbsp chopped parsley
1 tbsp vinegar
1-3 tsp lemon juice
salt and freshly ground pepper

Preheat the oven to 180°C/350°C. Place the tray you will be using for the vegetables in the oven to warm up.

Place the potatoes in a saucepan with cold water, add a pinch of salt and bring to the boil. Drain and wash with cold water.

Take the hot tray out of the oven, pour in 4 tablespoons of olive oil and season it with salt and pepper. Add the potatoes, carrots and turnips to one side of the tray and cover with the seasoned oil. Place the beets on the other side of the tray (do not mix with the potatoes and turnips) and roast everything for about 45 minutes. I usually do not peel the beets before roasting them so as to concentrate the flavor, but they can also be roasted peeled.

When the vegetables have been roasting for about 25 minutes, move on to preparing your steak.

Heat a frying pan until smoking hot. Pat the meat dry with a paper towel and season on both sides generously with salt and pepper; rub with a little sunflower oil. Add both steaks to the pan and press gently down so that they are fully in contact with the hot pan. Fry for 3-5 minutes, flip over and fry for another 3-5 minutes. 3 minutes on each side will give you a fairly rare steak; 5 minutes for medium to well done. When the steak is cooked, add the butter to the pan and pour it over the steak a couple of times while it is melting. This will improve the taste by adding nuttiness. Place the steak on a wooden board (or a plate), cover with foil and let it rest for 10-15 minutes (do not skip this part as it is essential to achieving a juicy steak)

Boil or steam the broccoli for 3-4 minutes. >>

Take the beets out of the oven, peel and quarter.

Finally, for the sauce (and just before serving), gently heat the olive oil in a saucepan and add the shallots, anchovies, capers and lemon zest. Heat for 1-2 minutes until warm, stir in the parsley and add a teaspoon of lemon juice and the vinegar before seasoning with black pepper and a little salt. Taste and adjust the seasoning.

Serve the steak with the roasted vegetables, the broccoli and the warm vinaigrette.

# Rusty ol' Steak

*I believe that classics exist for a reason and I don't see how we could live without steak in creamy sauce. When every single element is cooked to perfection it is the ultimate in indulgence and something meat lovers everywhere truly appreciate.*

*Time* | 1 hour     *Servings* | 4

4 beef steaks, at room temperature
salt and freshly ground pepper
sunflower oil to rub on the steaks

**Black pepper sauce**
1 tbsp extra virgin olive oil
2 onions, peeled and diced
80 ml/⅓ cup white wine
160 ml/⅔ cup chicken stock
120 ml/½ cup cream
1 tbsp black peppercorns, crushed
salt

**Crispy potatoes**
½ kg/18 oz potatoes, cut into wedges
2 tbsp olive oil
salt and freshly ground pepper
a few sprigs of fresh rosemary

**Glazed carrots**
1 tbsp extra virgin olive oil
1 knob of butter
3 garlic cloves, peeled, lightly crushed
450 g/1 lb thin carrots (about 4-5
    per person), peeled
a few sprigs of fresh thyme
a few sprigs of fresh rosemary
500 ml/2 cups chicken stock

Preheat the oven to 200°C/400°F. Place the tray in which you will be baking the potatoes in the oven to heat it up.

Place the potato wedges in a saucepan with cold water, bring to the boil, turn the heat down and leave to simmer for 5 minutes.

Drain the potatoes and then return them to the saucepan to steam off any remaining water.

Take the hot tray out of the oven, pour in the oil and toss the potato wedges around in it, season with salt and pepper and scatter a few sprigs of rosemary on top. Bake for about 35 minutes.

For the carrots, heat the oil and butter in a large frying pan, add the garlic cloves, carrots and fresh herbs, and fry for 2-3 minutes, shaking the pan frequently.

Add 80 ml/⅓ cup of stock to the pan and reduce until there is almost no liquid left. Repeat with the rest of the stock, adding about 80 ml/⅓ cup at a time. This may seem like a bit of a hassle, but it will allow you to build layers of flavor and achieve a tastier end result.

For the sauce, heat the oil in a saucepan and cook the onion on a medium-low heat for 5-7 minutes until soft.

Add the wine and continue to cook for a few more minutes, then add the stock and cook until the liquid has reduced by two thirds. Finally, stir in the cream and peppers.

For the steaks, heat a frying pan, preferably a cast iron one, until smoking hot. Season the meat with salt and pepper, rub with oil, then sear on all sides in the pan and place the pan in the oven (where the potatoes are still baking) for 3-5 minutes, depending on the size of the steaks and how well done you like your meat to be. Once the steaks are out of the oven, wrap them in foil and leave to rest for 3-5 minutes.

Just before serving, unwrap the steaks, add all the meat juices to the sauce and give it a good stir.

# Daube with beef cheeks

*Daube is a wonderfully aromatic stew with ancient roots in Provence. The meat is allowed to sit comfortably for hours soaking up the wine marinade before it is transferred to a casserole to cook for another eternity until the meat is falling apart and the scents wafting from the kitchen can bring even the most stubborn eaters to their knees. Throughout Provence you will find endless variations of daube using lamb or beef but my favorite cut for this dish is beef cheeks, which have the most flavor and were simply designed to be used in stews like this one. The end result reminds one of a boeuf bourguignon enriched with Mediterranean flavors, although even attempting to compare daube with boeuf bourguignon is wrong in more ways than I can ever describe (and would undoubtedly get me into terrible trouble during my next family visit). So let's just say that this is a marvelous stew, made for those like me who regard anything that has been simmered for hours in red wine to be nothing short of perfection.*

Time | 3 hours 20 mins     Servings | 4

800 g/28 oz beef cheeks
2 large onions, cut into 8 wedges
4 carrots, sliced into chunks
4 garlic cloves, chopped
1 bottle red wine (750 ml/3 cups)
2 tbsp olive oil
100 g/3½ oz flour
50 g/2 oz pancetta, chopped
2 tbsp tomato paste
2 tsp dried lavender buds
1 cinnamon stick
zest of 1 orange
30 g/1 oz black olives
salt and freshly ground pepper

**Bouquet garni**
1 bay leaf
a few sprigs of rosemary springs
a few sprigs of thyme
a few stalks of parsley

Marinate the beef cheeks with the onions, carrots, garlic and the wine, cover, and leave in the fridge for at least a few hours; overnight would be even better.

Before cooking, drain off and reserve the marinade. Pat the beef dry and coat with flour.

Heat a large casserole, add the olive oil and brown the beef cheeks an all sides. Remove from the casserole and set aside. Add the vegetables from the marinade and the pancetta to the casserole. Toss around for a few minutes on a high heat, then stir in the tomato paste and add the reserved wine, lavender, cinnamon, orange zest and olives and season with salt and pepper.

Return the beef cheeks to the pot, add the bouquet garni and allow everything to simmer gently. Cover tightly and leave to cook on a low heat for about 3 hours until the beef cheeks are tender. Taste and adjust the seasoning. If there is too much liquid, remove the lid, turn the heat up, and let it all cook a little longer.

Serve with boiled potatoes or roasted Jerusalem artichokes (see page 91).

# Blanquette de veau

*I usually start making blanquette de veau when the first frost starts to bite my cheeks, and it is a friend that stays with me the whole winter long. Quite the opposite to rich red wine stews, blanquette de veau has the most delicate flavors and an exceptionally tender veal, and it is one of those magical dishes where a few simple ingredients and a little time always result in something very special..*

Time | 2 hours 40 mins     Servings | 4

1 kg veal shoulder or flank, cut into squares

3 medium-sized carrots, halved and quartered

1 onion, peeled and halved

5 garlic cloves, halved

1½ 1/6 cups chicken stock

150 g/5½ oz pearl onions, peeled

250 g/9 oz button mushrooms

250 ml/1 cup cream

3 egg yolks

salt and freshly ground pepper

1-3 teaspoons fresh lemon juice

fresh pasta  (see page 114)

**Bouquet garni**

⅓ celery stalk

1 bay leaf

a few sprigs of thyme

a few parsley stalks

Put the veal in a large saucepan together with the carrots, garlic, onion and bouquet garni and cover with chicken stock. Bring everything to the boil and then reduce the heat.

Simmer the stew for 1½ hours, skimming away and discarding any scum from the surface. Add the pearl onions and continue to cook for another 30 minutes. Toss in the button mushrooms and cook for 20 minutes more.

Remove the bouquet garni, garlic and onion halves and then pour the stew through a colander, reserving the liquid.

Return the liquid to the heat and bring back to the boil before straining though a fine sieve.

Beat together the cream and egg yolks, stir in the stock and return to the heat. Continue to cook on a medium heat for a few minutes until the sauce thickens a little and coats the back of a wooden spoon when dipped in.

Remove from the heat, taste and adjust the seasoning if required, finishing off with a dash of lemon juice to bring out the flavor. Add the veal and vegetables to the sauce and serve with fresh pasta.

# Beef braised with tomato and oregano

*I love braising stuff in tomato almost as much as in wine. Be generous with the oregano here - it marries the tomatoes and beef beautifully and makes this stew both hearty and fresh.*

Time | 3 hours    Servings | 6

1 kg/35 oz beef, cut into chunks
   preferably chuck or beef cheeks
2 tbsp extra virgin olive oil
100 g/3½ oz flour
½ teaspoon each of salt and freshly
   ground black pepper
2 large onions, halved and sliced
1 carrot, sliced
5 garlic cloves
100 ml/½ cup white wine (optional)
2 x 400 g/14 oz canned tomatoes
250 ml/1 cup beef stock
pinch of sugar
4 tablespoons fresh chopped or 2
   tablespoons dried oregano
1 bay leaf

Heat the oil in a casserole. Season the flour with salt and pepper, coat the beef in the flour and brown on all sides; set aside.

Using the same pan, add more oil if needed and fry the onions on a medium-high heat, stirring all the time, until lightly caramelized. Stir in the carrot and garlic and cook for a few more minutes. Deglaze with white wine (if using) and dislodge all the bits stuck to the bottom.

Add the tomatoes, stock, oregano, sugar and the bay leaf and return the browned beef to the pan. Cover and leave to simmer for about 2½-3 hours until the meat is very tender. Halfway through, taste the sauce and adjust the seasoning; you may need more salt, pepper or even sugar. Serve with potatoes or just plain crusty bread.

# Roast leg of lamb with fennel and cherry madeira sauce

*I can barely imagine a more perfect dish to celebrate spring than a generous leg of lamb adorned with rosemary and garlic slowly roasting in the oven. It fills the house with fresh and savory scents and always has us counting the minutes until it is ready to be served for Sunday lunch or when we have a gang over for dinner. This humble roast is wonderful when served with its pan juices only, but I just love it with cherry Madeira sauce. So if you can bare waiting a few minutes more I cannot recommend it highly enough. Roasted fennel is good enough to be eaten on its own and can be used in salads or as a side dish for other roasted or grilled meats.*

*Time* | 1 hour 30 mins (start the day before)    *Servings* | 6 - 8

1.5 kg/3 lb and 3 oz boneless leg of lamb, trimmed
salt and freshly ground black pepper
5 fat garlic cloves, chopped
2 lemons, zest and juice
3 tbsp chopped fresh rosemary
4 tbsp extra virgin olive oil

**Roasted fennel and potatoes**
450 g/1 lb new potatoes
4 fennel bulbs, halved and quartered
a few tbsp extra virgin olive oil
salt and freshly ground pepper
juice of ½ a lemon

**Garlic spinach**
a few tbsp extra virgin olive oil
3 garlic cloves, chopped
300 g/10½ oz spinach
salt and freshly ground pepper
1 tbsp white wine vinegar

Season the lamb with salt and pepper and leave it in the fridge overnight.

On the day of cooking, mix together the garlic, lemon juice and zest, rosemary and oil. Rub it all over the leg of lamb (inside and outside) then truss it tightly and leave in the fridge for at least 5 hours to marinate.

Preheat the oven to 230°C/450°F. Place the lamb on a roasting tray, pour over the marinade and roast for 15 minutes before reducing the temperature to 180°C/350°F. Roast for another 40 minutes.

Remove the lamb from the oven, cover with foil and a tea towel and let it rest for 45 minutes.

While the lamb is roasting, scrub the potatoes, put them in a large saucepan, cover with cold water, bring to the boil and simmer for a few minutes before draining. When you have taken the lamb out of the oven, turn the heat up to 200°C/400°C. Toss the potatoes with the fennel, oil and lemon juice; season with salt and pepper. Place on a large tray and roast for 45 minutes.

To make the cherry madeira sauce, heat 10 g/½ tbsp of butter in a saucepan and gently cook the shallot with rosemary for a few minutes, until softened. Stir in the madeira, turn the heat up and let it cook for another minute. Finally, add the chicken stock and cherry jam, season with pepper and cook until reduced by two thirds. Remove the sprig of

**Cherry Madeira sauce**
*25g/2½ tbsp butter*
*1 large shallot, chopped*
*1 sprig of rosemary*
*120 ml/½ cup Madeira*
*360 ml/1½ cups chicken stock*
*1 tbsp cherry jam*
*freshly ground black pepper*

rosemary, stir in the pan juices from the lamb and add 15g/1 tbsp of butter.

For the spinach, heat the oil in a large saucepan, cook the garlic for a minute, add the spinach and toss it around until just wilted. Season with a little salt, pepper and vinegar and remove from the heat.

Serve the leg of lamb with the roasted vegetables, garlic spinach and cherry madeira sauce.

la Petite
€
une
€ les 2

# Rosemary lamb braised in red wine

Whenever I am at the butchers and gazing over the cuts and pondering all the possibilities they present, there is always a voice somewhere inside my head whispering to me to make a stew, regardless of the season. And the whispers inevitably include the words 'wine' and 'rosemary' and 'lots of fresh bread for dipping in the lovely sauce'. I have to admit that I am rather impatient when it comes to cooking and I tend to banish everyone else from the kitchen when I'm busy. I take bite after bite, just to check the taste of course, and nibble constantly at things while they are simmering away to hoped-for perfection. Lamb has such a strong and lovely flavor that it can handle quite a few additions, but few things work as well as rosemary and this stew is even better when paired with a vegetable tian (see page 220).

Time | 3 ½ hour     Servings | 6 - 8

2 ½ kg/5 ½ lb lamb shoulder, cut into
    pieces
3 tbsp olive oil
salt and freshly ground pepper
2 large onions, diced
4 garlic cloves, chopped
5 medium-sized carrots, peeled and
    sliced into 3-4 pieces
1 heaped tbsp tomato paste
2 tbsp balsamic vinegar
1 bottle red wine (750 ml)
2 x 400 g/14 oz canned tomatoes
1 tbsp brown sugar
a very large bunch of rosemary
3 bay leaves

Heat a large casserole with 2 tbsp of oil. Season the lamb with salt and pepper and quickly brown on all sides. Depending on the size of your cuts, you may have to do this in several batches. Set aside.

In the same pot, sauté the onions for a few minutes until they soften and then add the garlic and carrots and cook for another few minutes. Stir in the tomato paste, coating all of the vegetables, followed by the balsamic vinegar. Finally, pour in the red wine, canned tomatoes and brown sugar and stir. Add the rosemary and bay leaves, cover, and leave to simmer for 3 hours.

After 3 hours you can either drain the liquid and boil it down rapidly to reduce by a half to two-thirds, or you can take the lid off after 2 ½ hours, increase the heat and allow the liquid to reduce more slowly. In any event, it is essential to reduce the sauce in order to concentrate the flavor. Return the meat to the casserole to warm it up; it will be very tender and falling off the bone. Serve with tian (see page 220), potatoes or fresh pasta (see page 114).

# Potato and goat's cheese gratin

*France is truly the country of gratins. Each and every region has countless variations on how to make a delicious dish using only a few vegetables and very little effort. This particular one is both comforting and refreshing and is excellent as a vegetarian option or as a side to plain meats.*

Time | 1 hour 40 mins     Servings | 4

½ kg/18 oz potatoes, thinly sliced
300 g/10½ oz soft goat's cheese
2 tbsp extra virgin olive oil
2 large onions, finely diced
3 garlic cloves, chopped
generous pinch of chili flakes
3 tbsp chopped fresh parsley
2 tbsp chopped fresh rosemary
1½ tbsp tomato paste
8 medium tomatoes, chopped
1 tsp sugar
salt and freshly ground pepper
bread for serving (ciabatta or baguette
   will work well)

## Green salad

a few handfuls of mixed salad leaves
1-2 cucumbers, sliced
2 tbsp extra virgin olive oil
1 tbsp lemon juice
grated zest of 1 lemon
salt and freshly ground pepper

Preheat the oven to 200°C/400°F.

Heat the oil in a pan and fry the onion until soft; add the garlic, chili, parsley and rosemary and fry for 1 minute more, then stir in the tomato pasta, chopped tomatoes and sugar. Season with salt and pepper and let it simmer for about 10 minutes. Taste and adjust the seasoning.

Cover the sliced potatoes with cold salted water and bring to the boil. Drain and pat dry. Pre-cooking the potatoes will shorten the baking time for the gratin, otherwise it might take up to a few hours to bake.

Make the gratin as follows: spoon some of the tomato sauce into the bottom of a casserole dish, followed by a layer of potatoes, half of the goat's cheese, another layer of potatoes, a layer of tomato sauce, another layer of potatoes and goat's cheese and continue layering with the rest of potatoes and tomato sauce before ending with tomato sauce on top.

Cover with foil and bake in the middle of the oven for 1 hour. Remove the foil, turn on the oven grill and cook for about 10 minutes more until you have a nice crust on top.

Serve immediately with green salad and bread.

For the salad, mix all the ingredients together just before serving.

# Chorizo-stuffed zucchini

*Throughout summer, zucchini is an ever-present guest in my kitchen. It inevitably makes its way into each and every salad or couscous dish I make, but nothing beats small, round, stuffed zucchinis, which are a must for summer entertaining. This is a hearty and spicy version that will sweep you away to the narrow streets of Spain in an instant, where robust scents are the beating heart of the towns and villages.*

*Time* | 1 hour      *Servings* | 4

4 round zucchinis

1 tbsp extra virgin olive oil

1 medium onion, halved and sliced

130 g/4½ oz spicy chorizo, diced

3 garlic cloves, chopped

1 large tomato, chopped

1 red bell pepper, halved, cored and sliced

1 tbsp chopped fresh parsley

bread for serving

## Tomato sauce

2 tbsp extra virgin olive oil

1 onion, finely chopped

2 garlic cloves, finely chopped

2 tbsp chopped parsley

1 tsp tomato paste

4 ripe tomatoes, finely chopped

Pinch of sugar

Salt and freshly ground pepper

Preheat the oven to 180°C/350°F.

Start by making the sauce. Heat 2 tbsp of oil in a saucepan and cook the finely chopped onion until softened; add the garlic and parsley and cook for 1 minute, then stir in the tomato paste, chopped tomatoes and sugar. Season with salt and pepper and let it simmer for 10 minutes.

Slice the tops or 'caps' off the zucchinis (don't throw them out!) and scoop out the flesh using a teaspoon; chop up roughly. In a separate frying pan, heat the oil and fry the onion with the chorizo and garlic for a few minutes until the onion has softened. Add the tomato and peppers and season with salt and pepper; cook for another 5 minutes. Add the zucchinis and parsley and cook for a few more minutes, taste and adjust the seasoning. Stuff the zucchinis with the chorizo filling and place the caps back on top.

In a shallow oven dish, spread the tomato sauce over the stuffed zucchinis and bake for 30 minutes. Serve hot with plenty of fresh bread..

*Tip* | If round zucchinis are not available, regular ones can be used instead; just slice them lengthwise.

# Pumpkin, sage and bacon tart

*Pumpkin and sage for me are quintessentially fall - comforting and elegant, nourishing and pretty. This savory tart is the very definition of comfort food made fancy and it makes for a lovely appetizer or snack during a dinner party. The pastry here is so thin that it melts immediately in your mouth, giving way to the taste of crunchy bacon buried in a creamy blue cheese blanket. A veritable feast for the senses.*

Time | 1½ hour      Servings | 4 - 6

shortcrust pastry *(see page 276)*
200 g/7 oz smoked bacon, diced
45g/3 tbsp unsalted butter
4 onions, cut in half and sliced
½ medium-sized butternut squash,
    diced
2 eggs
160 ml/⅔ cup cream
100 g/3½ oz gorgonzola cheese (or
    any other blue cheese)
salt and freshly ground pepper
a handful of fresh sage leaves,
    shredded

Preheat the oven to 200°C/400°F.

Roll out the dough to the thickness of a dime and use the rolling pin to transfer it into a 36 x 13 cm/14 x 5 inch tart base, carefully pressing it down.

Allow to rest for at least 20 minutes in the fridge. Once chilled, prick the bottom of the tart in a few spots with a fork.

Place a sheet of baking paper on top of the pastry and fill the form with beans or baking weights to prevent the pastry from rising. Bake for 15 minutes, remove the baking paper and weights and continue to bake for 10 more minutes.

To make the filling, heat a large frying pan and fry the diced bacon until it turns crispy. Remove with a slotted spoon onto a paper towel. Wipe the pan clean, melt the butter and fry the onions for 15-20 minutes on a medium heat until caramelized. If the pan is too dry add another knob of butter before adding the butternut squash. Continue to cook for 2-3 minutes more and set aside.

Beat the eggs with the cream and season with salt and pepper.

Spread the caramelized onions and squash on the tart base, sprinkle over the bacon, crumble the gorgonzola on top, and then pour over the eggs and finish with a generous amount of sage. Bake in the oven for 20-25 minutes. Serve hot or cold.

# Oeufs en meurette

*Eggs in a luscious red wine sauce are my quick fix whenever I find myself craving some boeuf bourguignon. Wine sauces do need time to develop their flavor and for this sauce the wine should be added in small batches and allowed to fully cook down and caramelize with the vegetables on the bottom, creating layers and layers of flavor. However, even when you add all the wine at the same time it makes a spectacular wine sauce. This dish is excellent for a dinner party, but also great for Sunday lunch, with some red wine, too, of course.*

*Time* | 1 hour 5 mins     *Servings* | 4

4-8 eggs
1 tsp olive oil
100 g/3½ oz lardons (bacon cubes)
1 medium-sized onion, diced
1 medium-sized carrot, diced
1 stick of celery, diced
beef trimmings (optional)
500 ml/2 cups red wine
250 ml/1 cups beef stock
45g/3 tbsp cold butter
Salt and freshly ground pepper
2 tbsp white wine vinegar
bread, toasted to serve

**Bouquet garni**
1 sprig of rosemary
a few sprigs of thyme springs
a few stalks of parsley
1 bay leaf

In a saucepan, heat the oil and fry the lardons on a medium-high heat for 2-3 minutes. Add the onion and continue to cook for another 5 minutes, stirring occasionally. Stir in the carrot, celery, beef trimmings (optional) and cook for a few more minutes. Finally, add the wine and stock, season with black pepper and add the bouquet garni. Leave the sauce to simmer for 35-45 minutes. It should reduce by about two-thirds. Before serving, remove the bouquet garni and whisk in the butter.

To poach the eggs, bring a few liters of water to the boil in a large shallow saucepan, stir in the vinegar and turn the heat down to low. The secret is to keep the temperature just a little below simmering, somewhere between 65°C-85°C.

Crack each egg into a small bowl and gently slide into the water. Cook for about 4 minutes and then remove with a slotted spoon onto a paper towel to dry.

Serve 1-2 eggs per person on toasted bread (a few minutes under a hot grill) with the warm sauce.

# Roasted pumpkin m'hanncha with chorizo crumble

*M'hanncha is the so-called Moroccan snake, which is usually served as a dessert, but its interesting shape also lends itself to a few alterations and surprising fillings. The unsung hero of this dish is butter, which binds and enhances the sweetness of pumpkin and makes it altogether wonderful. Even without chorizo this pumpkin snake cake is splendid and makes a great vegetarian main course.*

Time | 1 hour    Servings | 4

1 small pumpkin, peeled
120 g/8 tbsp butter, cubed
2 tbsp chopped parsley
4 garlic cloves, halved
salt and freshly ground pepper
4 sheets filo pastry, 45 x 30 cm/
    18 x 12 inches
15 g/½ oz sliced almonds
60 g/2½ oz chorizo
100 g/3½ oz Greek yogurt or
    labneh
2 tsp sumac

Preheat the oven to 220°C/430°F.

Cut the pumpkin into chunks and toss with 70 g/4½ tbsp butter, a tablespoon of chopped parsley and the garlic. Season with salt and pepper and roast for about 25 minutes until the pumpkin is soft. Make sure you check and turn the pumpkin a couple of times during roasting to be sure it is well coated in butter.

Once out of the oven, remove the garlic and, using a fork, mash the pumpkin with the butter and parsley. Taste and adjust the seasoning.

Turn the oven down to 180°C/350°F and then melt the remaining butter in a saucepan.

Place two filo sheets on top of each other. Spread half of the mashed pumpkin on one edge, then gently roll it up (into something that looks like a sausage), taking care not to tear the pastry, and finally shape it into a circle. Repeat with the remaining filo pastry and complete the circle by rolling it around and tucking in the ends. Brush generously with butter and sprinkle with half of the remaining parsley and almonds. Bake for about 20 minutes until the pastry is golden brown.

In the meantime, chop the chorizo and fry it in a pan until crisp. Transfer onto a paper towel to absorb any excess fat. I sometimes even grind chorizo to an almost dust-like texture, but it can also be served roughly crumbled.

Serve the pumpkin m'hanncha with the chorizo crumble, with the remaining parsley sprinkled on top, and with the yogurt mixed with sumac on the side.

# Caramelized onion and yogurt tart

To say that I am immensely fond of savory tarts would be something of an understatement. The allure of flaky pastry surrounding flavorsome pockets of cream as lightly as a cloud is impossible to resist. I bake tarts all year round using everything the market stalls have to offer, and this particular beauty is perfect for a picnic or as an appetizer or indeed for just about any kind of occasion.

Time | 1 hour     Servings | 4

shortcrust pastry (see page 276)
2 tbsp olive oil
2 small onions, sliced in rings
2 tsp brown sugar
3 eggs
160 g/5½ oz natural yogurt
salt and freshly ground pepper
130 g/4½ oz cherry tomatoes,
    halved

Preheat the oven to 200°C/400°F.

Roll out the pastry using a rolling pin and transfer to the 24 cm/9½ inch tart case and gently press it down. Allow to rest for at least 20 minutes in the fridge.

Prick the bottom of the tart in a couple of spots with a fork (do not prick before chilling!), cover the pastry with baking paper and fill with beans or baking weights to prevent the pastry from rising. Bake for 15 minutes, then remove the baking paper and weights and continue to bake for another 10 minutes.

While the pastry is baking, get started on the filling. Heat the oil in a skillet and slowly fry the onions for about 10 minutes, turning occasionally, until they start to caramelize. Then sprinkle with sugar and allow to caramelize fully for another few minutes.

Beat the eggs with the yogurt and season with salt and pepper. Once the pastry is out of the oven, add the caramelized onions and cherry tomatoes, pour over the beaten eggs and yogurt and bake for 25-35 minutes, depending on your oven. Serve hot or cold.

# Tian

*A layered vegetable dish is not only pretty to look at, it is also an excellent partner for grilled or roasted and even stewed meats. My version comes with a slight twist and deviates a little from tradition. Adding a balsamic shallot relish at the bottom of the tian gives a deeper, more profound flavor, and it goes perfectly with braised lamb or any other roast meat.*

Time | 3 hours     Servings | 4-6

1 tbsp olive oil
5 shallots, peeled, halved and sliced
7 tbsp balsamic vinegar
2 tbsp brown sugar
1 sprig of thyme (optional)
2 small zucchinis, thinly sliced
1 summer squash, thinly sliced
2 small eggplants, thinly sliced
5 tomatoes, thinly sliced
250 g/9 oz cherry tomatoes, halved
5 garlic cloves, halved
a few sprigs of oregano
a handful of basil leaves
extra virgin olive oil for drizzling
   on top
salt and freshly ground pepper

Preheat the oven to 130°C/265°F.

Heat the oil in a heavy based frying pan and sauté the shallots for 5-10 minutes.

Pour in the balsamic vinegar, sugar and thyme and continue cooking until the vinegar is almost gone. This will take another 10-15 minutes.

Spread the shallot relish on the bottom of an oven-proof dish and layer the zucchini, squash, eggplant and tomato slices. Scatter the cherry tomatoes, garlic halves and fresh herbs on top. Season with salt and pepper and drizzle with a little olive oil.

Cut a circle out of a sheet of baking paper, large enough to cover the vegetables, and bake for 2 hours. Then remove the baking paper and bake for another 30 minutes.

Serve hot.

# Chicory gratin

*I love how chicories slowly transform under heat, losing their bitterness and taking on a new and wholly unique flavor. When braised to perfection they can be eaten straight out of the pan or baked with potatoes in a smashing gratin.*

Time | 45 mins      Servings | 4

3 chicories, sliced lengthwise
30 g/2 tbsp butter
1 lemon, juice only
3 tbsp sugar
180 ml/¾ cup chicken stock
salt and freshly ground pepper
5-6 potatoes
breadcrumbs or Gruyere cheese, to
   sprinkle on top.

Melt the butter on a high heat with the sugar and lemon juice in a heavy based saucepan. Slice the chicories lengthwise and place cut-side down in the saucepan to caramelize for a few minutes.

Add the stock, cover, and simmer for 15-20 minutes. Taste and adjust the seasoning. While the chicories are braising, peel and slice the potatoes and boil for 10-15 minutes until done. Drain and return the saucepan to the heat to allow any excess moisture to evaporate.

Preheat the oven to 200°C/400°F.

Place the boiled potatoes in a baking dish, arrange the braised chicories on top, spoon in some of the braising liquid (the potatoes will soak it up while baking), sprinkle some breadcrumbs or Gruyere cheese on top and bake for 20-30 minutes. Serve hot as a side dish or as a vegetarian main course.

# Glorious desserts

◄▲►

I think the world would be a dark and hollow place if sweets, especially chocolate, were to somehow suddenly disappear. Desserts have always had a special place in my heart and I firmly believe that no matter how filling a meal has been there is always enough room for dessert.

# Vanilla yogurt panna cotta

*I rarely order panna cotta when eating out, especially the vanilla variety, but it is one of my favorite desserts to make at home and this is perhaps one of the best panna cottas out there: creamy and rich but still light enough at the same time. The humble vanilla flavor really shines when used generously and the cherry blueberry sauce is delicious enough to be bottled and used every time jam is needed. Actually, this panna cotta is fantastic with just about any fruit or berries on top, as long as they provide the right contrast to the creamy base.*

**Time** | 15 mins    **Servings** | 4

250 ml/1 cup cream
2 vanilla pods, seeds scraped out
2½ leaves golden gelatin
2 tbsp honey
250 g/9 oz Greek yogurt

**Cherry blueberry sauce**
125 g/4½ oz blueberries
1 tsp sugar
2 tbsp Crème de cassis
250 g/9 oz fresh or frozen cherries

Combine the cream with the vanilla seeds and cook gently in order to allow the vanilla to infuse.

Soak the gelatin leaves in ice-cold water for 5 minutes. When the cream reaches boiling point, remove from the heat, squeeze the water out of the gelatin leaves and quickly stir into the cream.

Pour the mixture into a jug and leave to cool down for 5 minutes. Stir in the honey until it has fully dissolved, add the Greek yogurt and divide between 4 glasses. Leave to set for at least 4 hours in the fridge.

To make the cherry blueberry sauce, heat the blueberries with the sugar and the Crème de Cassis for a few minutes until the blueberries start to 'pop', then stir in cherries and cook for a few more minutes until the sauce has thickened.

# Chocolate banana ice cream

*When the heat of summer reaches its peak this is how I like to start my days: with a slightly modified Sicilian breakfast. In fact, if I weren't in the habit of making this ice cream over and over again for dessert after lunch and sometimes dinner, it would definitely have ended up in the breakfast treats section. Blending frozen bananas gives the creamiest of ice cream without having to add sugar or cream. Freezing ripens bananas and enhances their natural sweetness and they then only need to be blended until they are smooth and creamy. This might take a few minutes, depending on how strong your blender is, but your patience will be richly rewarded. I think it is best served immediately, but you can also freeze it again and serve at a later date.*

Time | 5 mins     Servings | 2

3 bananas

2 heaped tablespoons of unsweetened
   raw cacao

1 tbsp coffee liquor (optional)

a handful of fresh strawberries
   (optional)

Peel and slice the bananas. Place them in a shallow dish and freeze.
Once the bananas are completely frozen, blend them until smooth. This may take a few minutes and might require a bit of scraping of the sides. Once they are nice and smooth, add the cacao powder and the liquor and blend until these are fully incorporated.
Serve immediately with fresh strawberries or freeze again.

# Yogurt and pomegranate verrines

*We often make this during the week at home when a simple and healthy dessert is called for. It is fresh, bright and delicious and doesn't feel like something particularly healthy, though it most certainly is. Labneh is a permanent resident in my fridge that I prefer to use whenever I am making verrines because of its thicker texture. But Greek yogurt works just as well, too.*

Time | 10 mins     Servings | 2

1 pomegranate
250 g/9 oz Greek yogurt or labneh
2 tbsp orange juice
½ tsp orange zest
1-2 tsp honey
a few tablespoons of chopped
   pistachios

Slice the top and bottom off the pomegranate and make 2-3 shallow incisions in the fruit. In a large bowl filled with cold water, tear the pomegranate apart and carefully release the seeds. Drain and dry on a paper towel.

Combine the yogurt, juice, zest and honey

Layer the yogurt cream with the pomegranates in serving glasses or bowls (verrines) and top off with pistachios before serving.

# Chocolate cherry ice cream

Perched on a mountaintop, overlooking the sea and often hidden in the clouds, entering the town of Erice is like emerging into a dream. Its streets are paved with cobblestones and clutched between ancient structures that have not yet been touched by modern hands. One could be forgiven for thinking that medieval ghosts are possibly the only inhabitants of the narrow streets that lead to the spot where a temple built for the goddess Venus once stood. Lost among these ancient streets are tiny little pastry shops that boast what many consider to be the best cannoli in all of Sicily: crunchy and creamy and likely to steal a little bit of your heart forever with each bite. The delicious ricotta cannoli filling was the inspiration for this ice cream, one that brings with it snippets of my favorite Sicilian dessert in the heat of summer.

Time | 15 mins    Servings | 4

400 g/14 oz full-fat Greek yogurt
150 g/5½ oz sheep's milk ricotta
  cheese (or regular ricotta if you
  cannot find it)
2 vanilla pods, seeds scraped out
2-3 tbsp honey
150 g/5½ oz chopped fresh cherries
2 tbsp grated dark chocolate,
  preferably min. 70% cacao

Combine the yogurt, ricotta and vanilla seeds. Sweeten with honey according to taste and either pour it into the ice cream machine or place it in the freezer, mixing thoroughly every 30 minutes for 2-3 hours.
Before finally freezing the ice cream, stir in the cherries and grated chocolate. Remove from the freezer at least 10 minutes before serving.

# Red wine strawberry eton mess

My father-in-law tells the story of how as children they would often eagerly count the minutes until morning when the ripest of strawberries would be awaiting them after spending a night soaking in red wine. It is perhaps one of France's best-guarded secrets. Something magical happens to strawberries when they are soaked in wine and some stronger booze, deepening their already heavenly flavor. Served on top of a fluffy cream with crunchy meringue, it is a dessert that is sure to excite the senses.

*Time* | 15 mins (start the day before)      *Servings* | 4

1 tbsp Grand Marnier
2 tbsp sugar
80 ml/⅓ cup red wine
250 g/9 oz ripe strawberries, halved

**Eton mess**
350 ml/1½ cups cream, chilled
1 vanilla pod, seeds scraped out
a few handfuls of meringues, lightly
  crushed (see page 244)

Mix the Grand Marnier with the sugar and red wine, pour it over the strawberries, cover, and chill in the fridge overnight.

Whip the cream with the vanilla until it forms into stiff peaks, then gently fold in the lightly crushed meringues and a few tablespoons of strawberries.

Divide between 4 glasses and top off with strawberries soaked in red wine.

*Tip* | Do not pour all the wine from the soaked strawberries onto the dessert as this will make it too watery.

# Plums in spicy wine and mascarpone

*This dessert reminds me of a good mulled wine because of its bite and I can hardly wait to make it each time fall comes around. A light touch of cold mascarpone, which melts like ice cream, is all that is needed here to cut through the richness of the wine sauce. A truly perfect dessert..*

Time | 1 hour     Servings | 4

250 g/9 oz mascarpone cheese

1 vanilla pod, seeds scraped out

2 tsp powdered sugar

30 g/2 tbsp unsalted butter

zest and juice of 1 orange

4 tbsp sugar

1 cinnamon stick

350 ml/1½ cups red wine (more if needed)

4-8 firm purple plums, halved and diced

Spilt the vanilla pod, scrape out the seeds and mix with the mascarpone and powdered sugar; set aside.

Heat a large heavy based pan and melt the butter. Add 1 tbsp of orange juice and the sugar, allow the sugar to melt and give it a few minutes to caramelize.

Add the rest of the orange juice, the orange zest, leftover vanilla pod, cinnamon stick and red wine. The red wine should cover the plums up to more than halfway, though it is even better when they are fully submerged, but if you don't want to waste that much wine or have already consumed the rest while cooking, no worries; just turn the plums a couple of times while they are cooking.

Allow the whole lot to simmer for about 15 minutes or until the plums are soft and almost melting. Remove them from the pan and reduce the sauce until only a few tablespoons remain.

Before removing the sauce from the heat, check whether you are happy with the taste balance and add a bit more sugar or orange juice if needed and heat again. Return the plums to the pan to warm them up and serve with vanilla mascarpone cream.

# Labneh cheesecakes

*I love making desserts in a glass. For me, it is the perfect way of presenting a lovely sweet dessert with the minimum of fuss, and these little cheesecakes can be made very swiftly. Labneh is a wonderful alternative to cream cheese and results in a slightly lighter texture, but regular cream cheese will do the job here too.*

*Time* | 15 mins    *Servings* | 4

*1 large ripe mango*
*2-3 limes, zest and juice*
*200 ml/¾ cup cream, chilled*
*250 g/9 oz labneh or cream cheese*
*2-4 tbsp powdered sugar*
*100 g/3½ oz digestive biscuits*
*200 g/7 oz raspberries*

Crumble the biscuits and set aside.

Blend the mango with a little lime juice.

Beat the cream with the labneh, grated lime zest and sugar and another drop of lime juice. Taste and add more lime juice or sugar if needed.

Take four glasses and layer with the crumbed biscuits and lime cream, finishing off with the mango coulis and raspberries.

# Double chocolate panna cotta

*This panna cotta is not a light affair by any means and one I tend to reserve for very special occasions. The lemon zest cuts wonderfully through the almost over-the-top sweetness of the white chocolate, though the panna cotta still stays rich and chocolaty. I also tend to be quite liberal when it comes to pouring in the Grand Marnier, which makes for a boozy, almost bitter dark chocolate cream that offers the perfect contrast to the white chocolate panna cotta in this chocolate lover's delight.*

*Time* | 20 mins (start the day before)    *Servings* | 4-6

360 ml/1½ cups cream
160 ml/⅔ cup milk
1 lemon, zest only
2½ golden gelatin leaves
100 g/3½ oz white chocolate, chopped

**Dark chocolate cream**
50 g/2 oz dark chocolate, preferably 70% cacao
2-3 tbsp milk
120 ml/½ cup cream, chilled
1 tbsp Grand Marnier

In a saucepan, slowly simmer the cream, milk and zest. Set aside to infuse for 5-10 minutes. Strain through a fine sieve and return to a low heat again.

In the meantime, soak the gelatin leaves in cold water for 5 minutes. When ready, squeeze out the extra water and stir into the hot cream mixture, quickly followed by the white chocolate, stirring vigorously all the time until you have a homogenous cream. Divide between 4 glasses or molds and leave in the fridge to set for 4-6 hours; overnight works best.

Before serving, melt the chocolate in a bowl over hot water and then stir in the milk. Let it cool down a little before stirring in the Grand Marnier. Whip the cream until it forms soft peaks and then stir it into the melted chocolate.

Top the white chocolate panna cotta with the dark chocolate cream and serve.

# Rose meringues

*Rose petals add wonderful flowery notes to these little gems without overpowering them or making them too 'soapy' in taste, which can sometimes happen when working with flowers. The meringues are great on their own, but are even better when sandwiched with raspberry cream. I tend to think that meringues need a fruity acid to cut through their sweetness. Together they make the perfect melt-in-your-mouth sweet.*

*Time* | 1 hour 15 mins     *Servings* | 4

2 egg whites, at room temperature
pinch of salt
115 g/4 oz/½ cup plus 1 tbsp caster
  sugar
1 tbsp crushed dried rose petals

**Raspberry cream**
120 ml/½ cup cream, chilled
1 vanilla pod, seeds scraped out
2 tsp caster sugar
200 g/7 oz raspberries

Preheat the oven to 120°C/250°F.

Beat the egg whites with a pinch of salt until stiff peaks start to form. Gradually add the sugar, beating vigorously as you do so. Continue to beat until the meringue looks thick and glossy, but do not overdo it. Pipe out mini meringues onto a tray lined with baking paper, sprinkle with the rose petals and bake for 1 hour. Then turn off the oven, open the door a bit, and let them cool down.

Chill the bowl in which you'll be whipping the cream. Add the vanilla seeds to the cream, along with the sugar, and whip until it forms stiff peaks.

Using your fingertips, break up the raspberries and fold them into the cream.

Spoon a little raspberry cream between the meringues to form a sandwich. Serve immediately or chill until needed.

# Pear, orange and rosemary tart

*There is a distinctive sweetness to the air that tags on the tail of each passing mistral in Provence. At the height of summer, when the sun is mighty and the air thick and intoxicatingly sweet with the scent of blooming rosemary, each breath feels like a taste of sunshine. When, in winter, the cold creeps in and the sun forgets to visit us as often, I make this tart to breathe light and warmth into the house and to reminisce on far-off sunny days.*

Time | 1 hour    Servings | 4

sweet pastry (see page 276)
2 tbsp chopped rosemary

**Caramelized pears**
2 conference pears
15g/1 tbsp butter
2 oranges, juice only
1½ tbsp honey

**Orange custard**
250 ml/1 cup whole milk
2 oranges, zest only
3 eggs
40 g/¼ cup minus 1 tbsp light
   brown sugar

Make the pastry according to the instructions on p 276, also adding the rosemary and sugar.

Preheat the oven to 200°C/400°F.

Roll out the pastry and press it into a 24 cm/9½ inch tart base. Leave in the fridge to rest for at least 20 minutes.

Take it out and prick the bottom of the tart in a few spots with a fork. Place a sheet of baking paper on top of the pastry and fill the form with beans or baking weights to prevent the pastry from rising and bake for 15 minutes.

After 15 minutes remove the baking paper and the beans or baking weights and continue to bake for another 10 minutes.

Peel the pears, halve and core. Melt the butter in a pan, add the pears cut-side down and cook them for a few minutes on a medium-high heat, turning them every now and then.

Add the orange juice and honey, cover partially, and let everything simmer for 10-15 minutes, turning occasionally, until the liquid has turned to caramel and the pears are fully coated. Let them cool a little before slicing.

To make the custard, heat the milk with the orange zest until almost bubbling, then set aside to infuse for about 10 minutes. Strain and simmer again.

Beat the eggs with the sugar, then pour in the milk while stirring vigorously.

Slice the pears and arrange them in the tart base. Skim the foam off the custard, then pour it on top of the pears and bake for about 25 minutes, depending on the oven.

# Thyme and fleur de sel chocolate chip cookies

An earthy tone, such as thyme, shines and flourishes in pastries and these cookies are no exception. They are moist and chewy, and the chocolate is further underlined with a touch of flour de del on top and fresh thyme leaves hidden in each mouthful. I dare say they are pretty addictive and actually a little less sweet than your average cookie, which allows all the flavors to really shine. In a sealed container, they'll keep for at least 5 days... I think...because I've never had a cookie survive that long in my house.

Time | 30 mins     Servings | 6

120 g/8 tbsp butter

130 g/4½ oz/½ cup plus 2 heaped tbsp light brown sugar

1 large egg

220 g/½ lb/1½ cups flour

¼ tsp soda

½ tsp baking powder

¼ tsp salt

100 g/3½ oz good quality dark chocolate, well chopped

2 tbsp fresh thyme leaves

fleur de sel for sprinkling

Preheat the oven to 190°C/375°F.

Line two trays with baking paper and set aside.

Cream the butter and sugar until light and fluffy, add the egg and whisk until incorporated.

Stir in the dry ingredients and whisk for another 3-5 minutes until the dough has formed. Fold in the dark chocolate and thyme.

Using a small ice cream scoop or two teaspoons, scoop the dough onto the lined trays, flatten out a little, leaving enough space between cookies, sprinkle with a little fleur de sel and bake for 8 minutes.

Once out of the oven, let the cookies cool down for a few minutes on a rack and enjoy them warm with a cup of tea.

# Blueberry cream puffs

*I am not certain when exactly cream puffs went out of fashion, but they are an undeservedly forgotten treat. What is there not to like about golden pastry filled with silky cream? Choux pastry, the essential constituent of cream puffs, may sound fancy but it is one of the easiest things to bake, and without all too much effort you will soon have little bites of heaven in your hands.*

Time | 1 hour     Servings | 8

100 g/9½ tbsp butter
125ml/½ cup plus 1 tsp water
125 ml/½ cup plus 1 tsp milk
pinch of salt
150 g/5½ oz/1 cup flour
4 eggs

**Filling**
125g/4½ oz fresh or frozen
    blueberries
500 ml/2 cups whipped cream,
    chilled
3-4 tablespoons sugar

**Topping**
100 g/3½ oz dark chocolate,
    chopped
4 tbsp cream
Dried rose petals (optional)

Preheat the oven to 220°C/430°F and chill the bowl you will be using to whip the cream.

To make the choux pastry, melt the butter with the water and milk in a large saucepan. Heat to boiling point and tip in the salt and flour. Using a wooden spoon, beat everything briskly for up to 30 seconds until the dough no longer sticks to the sides of the saucepan. Allow to cool to room temperature (about 10 minutes).

While the dough is cooling, line 2 trays with baking paper. When the dough has cooled, beat in the eggs one at the time until the dough is smooth and glossy.

Pour the dough into a pastry bag and pipe out profiteroles about the size of a walnut, leaving enough space between for them to rise. If you do not have a pastry bag, spoon out the dough using two teaspoons.

Dip your fingers in cold water and smoothen out the surface of the profiteroles, as any spikes that protrude are likely to burn.

Bake the profiteroles for 10 minutes, then turn the oven down to 190°C/375°F and bake for another 15-20 minutes until golden brown.

Using a knife, poke a hole in the bottom of each profiterole to let out the steam (and to fill later) and leave them to cool on a rack.

To make the filling, blend the blueberries, whip the cream with the sugar until stiff peaks form and then fold into the blueberry sauce. Pour the cream into a piping bag and fill the profiteroles through the holes you have made.

To finish, melt the chocolate and cream together in a bowl over boiling water. Dip the profiteroles into the chocolate ganache and sprinkle with rose petals.

# Clafoutis with peach and lemon verbena

*Lavender may be the most famous herb in Provence, but for me it is the thought of lemon verbena that always brings back fond memories of my time there. It betrays hints of citrus and all the other aromas native to Provence, and every dish made using it feels warm, summery and that little bit extra special. You can also make tea with it, infuse it in panna cottas or even use it to bake a fragrant peach clafoutis. The subtle taste of peaches compliments the freshness of lemon verbena beautifully, resulting in a delicate dessert that is very easy to make.*

**Time** | 50 mins     **Servings** | 4

120 ml/½ cup milk

120 ml/½ cup cream

a handful of fresh lemon verbena
   leaves, roughly chopped

butter for greasing

3 tbsp sugar

2 large peaches or 4 small ones,
   peeled, halved and sliced

3 eggs

3 tbsp flour

pinch of salt

20 g/1½ tbsp butter, melted

powdered sugar for sprinkling

Preheat the oven to 180°C/350°F.

In a saucepan, slowly heat the milk, cream and lemon verbena, allowing it to infuse for at least 10 minutes on the heat.

Generously butter 4 oven-proof ceramic dishes (or 1 large one) and sprinkle in some sugar.

Arrange the sliced peach halves on the bottom.

Gently beat the eggs and sugar until creamy. Stir in the salt and flour.

Once the cream and milk have infused, strain and then slowly stir the milk-cream and melted butter into the batter

Pour the batter over the peaches and bake for about 35 minutes.

Dust with powdered sugar if you like and serve warm.

**Tip** | *If you cannot find fresh lemon verbena, the dried variety will do.*

# Apple and ricotta crostata

When you feel you've nearly had your fill of apples for one season, this rustic tart is great for dessert and sometimes even a fancy breakfast. Orange blossom water imparts fantastic aromas and flavor and, according to legend, it possesses calming qualities and treats made with it were often given to children to ease a bad temper.

Time | 1 hour    Servings | 2-4

sweet pastry (see page 276)
3 large apples
1 tbsp lemon juice
250 g/9 oz ricotta
2 tbsp orange blossom water
1 vanilla pod, seeds scraped out
2 tbsp sugar, plus extra for sprinkling
1 egg yolk
1 tbsp honey

**Egg wash**
1 egg
1 tbsp water

Preheat the oven to 220°C/430°F.

Peel, half and core the apples, then slice them as thinly as you can and pour over the lemon juice. Set aside.

Mix the ricotta with the sugar, orange blossom water, vanilla seeds and egg yolk. Set aside.

Roll out the pastry fairly thin on a sheet of baking paper. Spread the ricotta cream onto the pastry, leaving about 3 cm free on each side. Arrange the apples as neatly or as haphazardly as you like and fold up the pastry sides.

Heat the honey a little until it becomes very fluid and use a pastry brush to spread it on top of the apples.

Beat the egg with the water and brush on the folded pastry.

Finish by sprinkling sugar all over.

Transfer the baking paper with the crostata onto a baking tray and bake for 15 minutes and then reduce the temperature to 200°C/400°F and continue to bake for another 20-30 minutes.

# Red wine custard tartlets

*My love for red wine transcends savories and touches sweets too, providing them with depth and character. This weird-sounding tart is actually a forgotten French classic and is incredibly delicious and easy to make. Reduced spiced red wine gives an almost chocolate-like flavor and the red wine sweeps through each bite in waves. It is both subtle and unique and quite unlike any other dessert I know. One of my all-time favorites.*

*Time* | 2 hours    *Servings* | 6

sweet pastry (see page 276)
600 ml/2½ cups red wine
1 cinnamon stick
1 vanilla pod
zest of ½ an orange
3 eggs
60 g/¼ cup plus 1 tbsp sugar

Preheat the oven to 200°C/400°F.

Roll out the pastry to the thickness of a dime, measure and cut out circles for 6 tartlet bases (with removable bottoms), plus an additional 1cm extra for each one, and press them into the tartlet bases. Allow them to rest for at least 20 minutes in the fridge.

After that, prick the bottoms of the tartlet shells in a few spots with a fork, place a sheet of baking paper on top of the pastry and fill the forms with beans or baking weights to prevent the pastry from rising. Bake for 15 minutes, remove the baking paper and weights and continue to bake for another 5-10 minutes, depending on your oven.

For the red wine custard, simmer the red wine with the vanilla, cinnamon and orange zest. Cook until the liquid is reduced by two thirds. This will take about 15-25 minutes. Strain the infused wine through a fine sieve and return to a low heat.

Beat the eggs with the sugar and then, stirring vigorously, slowly pour in the wine. Strain through a cloth to get rid of any foam, divide between the tartlet shells and bake in the oven for about 25 minutes, depending on your oven.

Allow to cool down completely before serving.

# Macarons

It was during my first Christmas in France, a good ten years ago I believe, when I first experienced the sight of a tray of lovely colored cookies being sent around the table until it was my turn to pick and try one. Love at first bite would probably best describe the sensation of tasting macarons for the very first time. And so an obsession was born, and on subsequent visits that tray full of little patisserie gems has never managed to stray far from my reach. The macaron is shrouded in myth and legend regarding the difficulty involved in achieving the perfect 'feet' and the crunchy, chewy texture for which macarons are famous. But really it's just another cookie, though a very good-looking one I might add, but still just a cookie, albeit with a couple of extra steps you need to follow and proportions that demand respect. Follow the instructions to the letter and you will end up with a beautiful delight fit for any occasion. I've included a couple of my own favorite fillings here, of which the jasmine white chocolate ganache is nothing short of divine, but all the others are fantastic as well.

*Time* | 1 hour 30 mins (begin preparations the day before)    *Servings* | 6-8

90 g/3¼ oz egg whites (about 3 egg whites), at room temperature
210 g/7½ oz powdered sugar
100 g/3½ oz almond flour (after sifting)
pinch of salt
35g/1¼ oz granulated sugar
¼-½ tsp powdered food coloring (optional)

**Jasmine and white chocolate ganache**
150 ml/⅔ cup minus 2 tsp cream
2 teaspoons of jasmine pearl tea
150 g/5½ oz white chocolate
60 g/4 tbsp butter

The night before: separate the egg yolks from the whites, place the whites in an airtight container (or cover with foil) and leave on the kitchen counter for 24 hours. DO NOT place them in the fridge.

On the day of cooking: preheat the oven to 100°C/212°F, pour the almond flour onto a sheet of baking paper and dry in the oven for about 10-15 minutes. This is especially important if your house is in any way humid, as macarons are quite sensitive to any additional moisture.

Mix the powdered sugar and almond flour together, sift again, and set aside.

Add a pinch of salt to the egg whites and beat them lightly until they start to foam. Add half of the granulated sugar and the food coloring, if using, and beat for a few minutes until well-combined and soft peaks have formed.

Add the rest of the granulated sugar and beat until you have a thick glossy mixture and stiff peaks, but don't overbeat it.

Stir in the dry ingredients, first breaking the merengue with a few quick strokes, and then gently mix with a spatula until well combined. Try to do this using no more than 10 strokes.

Using a dough scraper or the same spatula, fold the merengue until the batter is falling of the spatula and the 'ribbons' that form dissolve within a minute.

Pour the batter into a piping bag and pipe out rounds about 1.5 cm/

## Salted butter caramel

225g/½ lb/1 cup plus 2 tbsp white
    sugar
160 g/10½ tbsp salted butter
pinch of Fleur de Sel
120 ml/½ cup cream

## Vanilla orange cream cheese

1 vanilla pod
250 g/9 oz cream cheese
2 tsp orange juice
2 tbsp powdered sugar

½ inch in diameter. Let them rest for 30 minutes to an hour to allow a skin to form. The skin is needed for the macarons to get their "feet" and prevent them from cracking while rising. To check if the skin has formed properly, lightly tap the macarons and if they are no longer sticky then they are ready (don't forget to check the sides as well).

Bake the macarons in the oven at 160°C/320°F for 12 to 15 minutes. Different ovens tend to have different cooking times so the baking time may vary, and it is always a good idea to test (taste) one (or two) shells to check if they are done.

To make the jasmine and white chocolate ganache, gently heat the cream and add the jasmine tea. Cover and leave to infuse for 10 minutes. Strain, bring to the boil, and stir in the finely chopped chocolate. Use a hand-held blender or a whisk to combine everything until homogeneous and then remove from the heat and stir in the cold butter. Place in the fridge for about 30 minutes to thicken.

To make the salted butter caramel, melt the sugar in a saucepan on a low-medium heat. Be sure to use a saucepan that allows you to see the color of the sugar as it melts, otherwise you can easily burn it. When the sugar starts to melt (you will first see this happening at the sides) shake the pan occasionally to mix the sugar, but do not stir. When the caramel has acquired a nice dark amber color, take it off the heat and stir in the butter (careful here as it tends to splash), add a pinch of Fleur de Sel and, finally, stir in the cream. Transfer the caramel to a jar/container and leave it to cool to room temperature. Store it in the fridge until needed.

To make the vanilla orange cream cheese filling, split the vanilla pod, scrape out the seeds and add them to the cream cheese, together with the orange juice and sugar. If the cream cheese is too runny, leave it to set in the fridge for 1-2 hours.

Pour the macaron filling into a piping bag and pipe some of the cream onto a macaron shell and top with another shell. Repeat with the rest, then place the macarons in an airtight container and store for at least 24 hours in the fridge. This will allow the crunchy/chewy texture to develop. An hour or so before serving, take the macarons out of the fridge to bring them up to room temperature.

◄▲►

*Variation* | *Black sesame makes a fantastic macaron filling. Use the jasmine and white chocolate ganache recipe, but instead of the jasmine add 1 tablespoon of ground black sesame seeds and do not strain.*

# Flourless chocolate cake with cinnamon custard

*If chocolate was a religion I would most likely be amongst its most devoted followers, for it is a substance with the power to make our worldly worries seem of lesser importance. This cake has powers of its own too. It is extremely rich and even fudgy, and when a slice of it is lying in front of you nothing else really matters. Fluffy cream or ice cream is essential to this kind of cake, I'm afraid, and when the seasons turn colder cinnamon custard is simply irreplaceable.*

**Time** | 45 mins     **Servings** | 6

200 g/7 oz good quality dark
  chocolate
80 g/5½ tbsp butter, plus extra for
  greasing a baking tin
40 g/¼ cup sugar
4 eggs, separated
pinch of salt
zest of 1 orange (optional)
2 tbsp Grand Marnier (optional)

**Cinnamon custard or ice cream**
½ vanilla pod, seeds scraped out
1 cinnamon stick
250 ml/1 cup whole milk
80 ml/⅓ cup cream
2 egg yolks
2 tbsp sugar
1 teaspoon corn starch

Preheat the oven to 180°C/350°F.

Melt the chocolate and butter in a bowl over hot water, stirring every once in a while. It will take 2-4 minutes for the chocolate and butter to melt. Note: make sure that the water is not boiling or touching the bowl or the chocolate may start to cook. While the chocolate and butter are melting, grease an 18cm baking tin and set aside.

Once the chocolate has melted, remove the bowl from the hot water and stir in the sugar, followed by the egg yolks, one at a time. Finally, add the zest and Grand Marnier (if using).

Quickly whip the egg whites with a pinch of salt into stiff peaks. Gently fold the whipped egg whites into the chocolate batter, adding ⅓ of the whites at a time. Do not overbeat it.

Pour everything into the buttered tin and bake for 25-30 minutes and then allow to rest for 5-10 minutes before serving. For the cinnamon custard, split the vanilla pod and scrape out the seeds, add them (with the pod) to the milk and cream, together with the cinnamon stick.

Bring to a light simmer, remove from the heat and let everything infuse for 30 minutes, then strain and bring to a simmer again. Beat the egg yolks with the sugar and corn starch until fluffy and doubled in mass, then slowly pour in the milk, stirring vigorously all the time. Once all the milk is incorporated, return the custard to the heat and continue to cook on a medium-low heat, stirring all the time, until it coats the back of a wooden spoon. This will take about 5 minutes.

Pour into a jug and serve immediately with the chocolate cake.

◂▸

**Tip** | In summer time, the same custard can be poured into an ice cream maker to give you an incredibly delicate cinnamon ice cream. Just remember to skip the corn starch when making ice cream.

# Rhubarb and strawberry tart with pistachio frangipane

In early spring, when rhubarbs and strawberries come out together but the strawberries have not reached the peak of their taste and need a little help, baking them into a tart is my favorite way of using them. Pistachio frangipane has a much more distinctive flavor than an almond one and together with melting pastry, a thin layer of strawberry liquor jam and macerated rhubarb, it makes a tart that will definitely have you coming back for more.
Even though there are quite a few different elements to this dessert, it can all be done quite quickly and the actual hands-on work is minimal. So whenever you are hosting a special occasion or just want to spoil yourself with something truly special, go for this tart.

*Time* | 2 hours     *Servings* | 6

3 large rhubarb stalks, sliced in
   equal-sized pieces
250 g/9 oz strawberries, diced
1 vanilla pod, seeds scraped out
4 tbsp crème de cassis
2 tbsp sugar
sweet pastry (see page 276)

### Pistachio frangipane
150 g/10 tbsp butter
100 g/½ cup sugar
1 tbsp rose water
1 egg
150 g/5½ oz/1 cup plus 3 tbsp
   ground pistachios

Combine the rhubarb stalks, strawberries, vanilla, crème de cassis and sugar. Place in the fridge for 30 minutes to 1 hour.
Preheat the oven to 190°C/375°F.
Roll out the pastry and use the rolling pin to transfer it into the 36 x 13 cm/14 x 5 inch tart tin and gently press it down. Allow to rest in the fridge for at least 20 minutes.
Prick the bottom of the tart in a few spots with a fork (do not prick before chilling!), place a sheet of baking paper on top of the pastry and fill with beans or baking weights to prevent the pastry from rising. Bake for 15 minutes, remove the baking paper and weights, and continue to bake for another 10 minutes.
While the pastry is baking, set aside the rhubarb stalks and cook the strawberries in a saucepan with the crème de cassis for 15-20 minutes until you have a jam.
To make the pistachio frangipane, combine the butter and sugar in a food processor and blend for 1-2 minutes. Add the rosewater and egg and blend for one minute more. Finally, stir in the ground pistachios.
Spread the jam on the base of the tart, followed by the pistachio frangipane, and arrange the rhubarb on top. Bake for 25-30 minutes, depending on your oven.

# Almond cake with raspberries

This is a cake for a celebration, for marking moments of importance or creating new ones for the future. It is light and fresh, with the subtle flavors of lime and vanilla popping up in every bite. Using lime curd is optional but it makes for an even more special and clandestine treat, as it only reveals itself when sliced. It is best eaten on the day you make it, but it will keep for a few days in the fridge, though be sure to let it come up to room temperature before serving because it loses all its subtlety when eaten too cold.

**Time** | 1 hour 15 mins    **Servings** | 8 - 12

6 eggs

3 tbsp honey

zest of 2 limes, finely grated

90 g/3½ oz/¾ cup ground almonds (almond flour)

50 g/2 oz/⅓ cup flour

pinch of salt

butter for greasing the tin

300 g/10½ oz raspberries

### Lime curd

1 whole egg

2 egg yolks

100 g/½ cup sugar

pinch of salt

zest of 2 limes

60 ml/4 tbsp fresh lime juice

60 g/4 tbsp unsalted butter, cubed

### Mascarpone cream

250 ml/1 cup cream

250 g/9 oz mascarpone

1 tbsp powdered sugar

1 vanilla pod, seeds scraped out

Preheat the oven to 180°C/350°F.

Separate the egg yolks from the whites. Beat the eggs yolks with the honey and lime zest for a few minutes, stir in both types of flour and combine well.

In a separate bowl, beat the egg whites with a pinch of salt until soft peaks have formed and gently fold into the batter, ⅓ at a time.

Grease a round spring form (18cm/7 inches diameter) with butter and line the sides and bottom with baking paper. Pour in the batter and bake for 25-30 minutes; a wooden skewer inserted into the center of the cake should come out clean when done.

Let the cake cool for 10 minutes in the tin and then carefully remove it from the mold and leave it on a rack to cool completely.

For the curd, beat the eggs, sugar, salt and zest until the mix becomes pale and creamy, then stir in the lime juice and beat again.

Place the bowl over a pan of simmering water and stir continuously until the curd starts to thicken. This will take about 10 minutes. Remove the bowl from the water and quickly stir in the cold butter. Let it cool down. Beat the mascarpone with the cream, sugar and vanilla seeds.

To assemble, halve the cake, spread a few tablespoons of mascarpone cream on the bottom half, arrange a neat layer of raspberries on top and spoon over the lime curd, leaving about 2cm free on each side (otherwise the curd will spill over). Make a second layer and top with mascarpone cream. Finish with a neat layer of raspberries.

# Essentials

◀▶

*The things I cannot live without*

# Pastry

*These are my basic to-go recipes for shortcrust and sweet pastries that are used throughout this book in various tarts.*

**Time** | 45 mins

**Shortcrust pastry**
200 g/1⅓ cup flour
pinch of salt
1 tsp sugar
100 g/6½ tbsp butter
1 egg, lightly beaten

**Sweet pastry**
200 g/1⅓ cup flour
50 g/¼ cup sugar
Pinch of salt
105 g/7 tbsp butter
1 egg, lightly beaten

Combine the butter with the flour, sugar and salt in the food processor. Pulse everything for about 10 seconds until the mixture resembles breadcrumbs.
Add the beaten egg and continue pulsing until the dough starts to stick together.
Remove the dough from the food processor, transfer onto a working surface and press it together using the palms of your hands, but do not knead it.
Wrap the dough in plastic wrap and leave it to rest in a fridge for at least 30 minutes.

---

# Herby tomato sauce

*This incredibly fresh sauce can be made in minutes and has limitless applications. I use a lot of variations of this sauce throughout the book and there are many more still waiting to be discovered.*

**Time** | 50 mins    **Servings** | 4

1 tbsp extra virgin olive oil
1 shallot, chopped
1 garlic clove, chopped
1 pinch of dried chili
a few sprigs of rosemary, chopped
a few sprigs of thyme, leaves only
a few small sprigs of parsley, chopped
6 ripe tomatoes, chopped
pinch of sugar
salt and freshly ground pepper
4-6 basil leaves, chopped

Heat the olive oil in a pan and gently fry the shallot for a few minutes. Add the garlic, chili flakes, thyme, rosemary and parsley and continue to fry for another 30 seconds. Stir in the tomatoes, season with sugar, salt and pepper, and let it all cook on a medium heat for 10-15 minutes, stirring occasionally.
Before removing from the heat, check the seasoning - if it's too sour for your liking, add a little more sugar or salt and pepper as needed. Blend and finish off with fresh basil.

# ✤ Roasted garlic ✤

Roasting garlic turns an ordinary and rather harsh ingredient into a sweet and soft delight without any trace of the severe flavor or scent. It's good enough to be eaten straight out of the oven crushed on bread with some salt, pepper and olive oil (sprinkle the bread with cheese and place it under grill for a few minutes to make a great appetizer), but it doesn't end there. The uses to which roasted garlic can be put are literally limitless: to flavor dips, add to soups and sauces, etc.

*Time* | 55 mins

1-10 garlic bulbs (or as many as you like)
1-3 tbsp extra virgin olive oil
salt and freshly ground pepper
a few sprigs of fresh thyme (optional)
a few sprigs of fresh rosemary (optional)

Heat the oven to 180°C/350°F. Line a tray with baking paper and set aside.

Slice off the top of each garlic bulb and peel off the outer layer.

Rub with oil and drizzle some extra oil on the cut-side. Season with salt and pepper, scatter the herbs on top and bake for 35-50 minutes. Depending on your oven, it might take more or less time, so check after half an hour.

Garlic is fully roasted when it feels completely soft when pricked with a fork. If the tops of the bulbs are browning too quickly you can cover them with aluminum foil.

Once the garlic is roasted and has cooled down, it can be stored in an airtight container in the fridge for a few weeks.

# ✤ Labneh ✤

Labneh is basically drained yogurt, and the longer it is left to drain the creamier it gets. After about 72 hours it becomes almost hard and then other possibilities open up. I prefer to use sheep's yogurt to make labneh because it is creamier and more flavorsome. But of course regular or goat's cheese yogurt will do the job too.

*Time* | 5 mins    *Makes* | about 250 g

500 g yogurt/18 oz (preferably sheep's)

Place the yogurt in a double cloth-lined sieve and place in the fridge for at least 12 hours.

# Homemade ricotta

As a frequent visitor to Sicily and a firm lover of the island's cuisine, it was inevitable that I would fall completely for sweets and savories that use ricotta. In Sicily, ricotta can be found just about everywhere and it is extremely rich and creamy because it is made using local sheep's milk, an important quality that comes back to haunt me whenever I am trying to recreate these delicacies back at home. Fortunately, these days ricotta can be made at home in a matter of minutes and sheep's milk is becoming more and more readily available at organic shops and markets or directly from farmers. However, if sheep's milk is nowhere to be found, cow's milk will work well, too, and will make a better ricotta that any you will find on the shop shelf.

Time | 35 mins     Quantity | 300 g/4 cups

1 ¼ cups sheep's milk (or regular full-fat cow's milk)

¼ teaspoon salt

4 tbsp fresh lemon juice

Pour the milk into a saucepan and place on a low-medium heat, add the salt and give it a quick stir to help it dissolve.

Bring the milk to near boiling point; if you have a thermometer this will be at around 80°C/175°F.

Remove from the heat, add the lemon juice and stir for 10-15 seconds; curds will begin appearing immediately.

Cover the pot with a clean towel and let it rest for 30 minutes.

Place a muslin/cheese cloth over a colander and pour the cheese into it. Let it drain for a few minutes and your ricotta is ready. This recipe is good for around 300 g/10½ ounces of ricotta.

◀▶

Serving ideas | Ricotta & zucchini crostini: season fresh ricotta with salt, pepper and lemon zest, spoon some onto a toasted baguette slice and top with thin zucchini slices quickly fried in olive oil.

Serrano & ricotta bruschetta: season ricotta with pepper and lots of chopped parsley, spread it on toasted ciabatta and finish it off with Serrano ham and pine nuts quickly fried in 1 tablespoon olive oil and balsamic vinegar.

With radishes: roast trimmed and oil-tossed radishes in the oven at 220°C/430°F for about 40 minutes, turning occasionally. Serve with fresh ricotta, thyme and bread.

# Menu ideas

## Spring gathering

Fresh ricotta and zucchini crostini & vin d'orange
&
Roasted asparagus salad and avocado salad
&
Roast leg of lamb
&
Rhubarb & strawberry tart

## A sicilian midsummer breakfast

Chocolate banana ice cream
&
Chocolate cherry ice cream
&
Sicilian brioche
&
Coffee and fresh fruits on the side

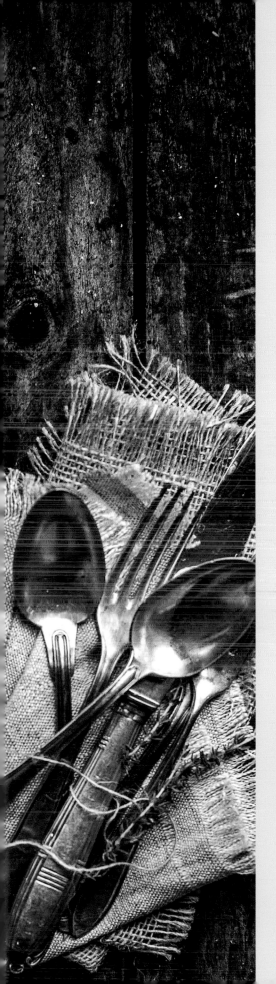

# Late summer tapas night

Kir royal & caponata

&

Roasted bell peppers

&

Smoked eggplant with mozzarella

&

Tomato carpaccio

&

Olive oil buns

&

Yogurt panna cottas

••••

# Autumn picnic

Mulled cider

&

Pumpkin, sage and bacon tart

&

Roasted chestnut and caramelized fennel soup

&

Chocolate cake with cinnamon custard

••••

# Winter feast

Salmon canapés & Lime and Prosecco punch

&

Chicken terrine with red wine onion jam

&

Tea-roasted chicken

&

Red wine tarts

&

Macarons

# Index

# Index

# Index

## Index